To Clark,
My dear [...]
see enough of...
Sincerely
Pam
xxxx

NOBLE FRIENDS

Pamela M. Dickson

Rocky

Fursman Kennels Ltd.

Pamela M. Dickson

Thank you to Dee Dee and Jay Hubbard of D.P. Systems, who rescued me right at the deadline for the printing.

Also, my thank-yous to Barbara Pegg, and Susan Burke, and especially to Jennifer, Cliff, and Jody for running the kennels so smoothly while I was putting this book together.

Jacket photos by Pamela M. Dickson.

In loving memory of my dear Mom and Dad.

NOBLE FRIENDS
Table of Contents

Chapter 1

Springhill Farm, Lower Penn

I have a small, rather battered, and much traveled suitcase which has stayed with me over the years and which contains pictures and newspaper articles of events I treasure-precious mementos carefully stored. I opened that suitcase today, and my thoughts went back to when I was a small child growing up in the West Midlands of England.

As I gazed out of the window in the breakfast room of the small cottage where I now live in Middleburg, Virginia, I marveled at the incredible beauty of the Virginia countryside-so similar in many ways to England. The oak trees, some over one hundred years old; the foxgloves, hollyhocks, roses, sweet williams, and violets flowering outside my window....they could so easily have been part of an English garden. I recalled the first flowers of spring in England, the snowdrops showing their shy heads in the woods, and later the carpet of bluebells massed beneath the trees. Then May, and the glorious smell from the white flowers of the hawthorn bush, and later, blackberrying in August with my sister Audrey.

We were a closely knit family with six children; I was the baby, with three elder sisters and two elder brothers. My parents ran a mixed farm named Springhill, set in the heart of the Midlands, not too far from the home of the famous Staffordshire china. We grew crops and had cattle, pigs, chickens, horses, dogs, ducks, geese, and turkeys.

Like many small children, I thought my Dad was the perfect father. He seemed to know so much about everything. All during my youthful career with horses and dogs, he was my trainer and teacher. Dad was over six feet tall, and well built, with dark hair and smiling hazel eyes. I do not remember him ever showing anger at any time. We were a houseful of children, but Dad was always tolerant and kind. I learned at an early age that he had been born with a weak heart, and this worried me.

Mom was just over five feet tall, small-boned and on the plump side. She had a pretty face, with fair hair and green eyes. A wonderful homemaker, she was always busy cooking, knitting, and sewing. She was mad keen for her garden, a passion which I have inherited. In the autumn we all helped to pick the plums, damsons, and cherries which she bottled. Mom always wore an apron, which she hastily took off whenever someone came to the front door.

We lived in an early 18th-century brick farmhouse with beautiful oak beams in most of the ceilings. A short distance from the house were the farm buildings with their cobbled yard. Looking to the right there was an arched brick cart shed with a touch of half timbering. Straight ahead was a range of buildings for storage and livestock, with a stable beyond. All the buildings were surrounded by a six-foot-high brick wall and were situated amidst a green checkerboard of undulating fields in this beautiful part of England.

Growing up here was an ideal life for a child. We had television, but seldom watched it, much preferring to be outside helping on the farm, riding, reading, and playing among ourselves. The popular games were Ring-a-Ring-o'-Roses, Nuts in May, Hunt the Slipper, and Hopscotch, often played at birthday parties given by local families. I rarely played with dolls, but was devoted to a teddy bear given to me by my sister Irene, when my brother John and I had scarlet fever and were both rushed off to hospital.

One of my earliest memories, back when I was only about four years old, is my Dad tossing me up on the back of one of the carthorses on their return home after a day's work in the fields. We had two large Suffolk draft horses, Bonny and Flower. Flower, with a bright white blaze on her magnificent chestnut head and four white socks, was the one I rode quietly back home. She was a special horse, being nearly blind, but she walked unhesitatingly over the fields, only stepping a little higher when she came to the gateways or was walking over areas less familiar. Those rides on Flower were the start of my lifelong love of animals.

Horse and man were a traditional partnership for the ploughing and harrowing of the fields, and there was perfect understanding between them as they worked. From early childhood I recollect the great plodding hooves and measured gait of our beloved carthorses.

Springhill Farmhouse, built in the 18th century.
Pictured, my sister Audrey with my niece, Christine, and Lassie.

The village smithy was a fascinating place to visit in my childhood. The muscular blacksmith would use his bellows to generate terrific heat from his furnace to forge the metal for the shoes. He used a hand-hammer and various hand tools to expertly shape the large shoes to fit the carthorses. I would delight in my visits there but always kept a respectful distance from the furnace. Today, even in rural England, carthorses have been replaced by tractors. Garages and repair shops have now taken the place of the village smithy.

The nearby village shop sold a medley of things, from milk, vegetables, and stamps to cough medicines, newspapers, cards, shampoo, and delicious sweets.

The shop was a magnet attracting our weekly pocket money. We would gaze in through the window, taking our time to decide which of the sticky sweets to choose. Then the kind shopkeeper would carefully weigh out the chosen sweets and hand over the package to small, grubby, eagerly waiting hands.

St. Anne's was our village church, built in 1650 out of local stone and with a slate roof. It was a small but extremely beautiful church with stained glass windows and old wooden pews which held about 40 people.

The pub, the Greyhound, was a popular meeting place for the locals. It was built in the 1800s of oak logs and stucco, with heavy oak beams set in the low ceilings and whitewashed walls. Over the open fireplace was a massive wooden mantel blackened by the smoke of many fires. A fox's head looked down with a glassy stare, oblivious to the antlered deer heads adorning the walls. Numerous horse brasses hung on either side of the fireplace. The flickering flames gleamed on the old copper kettle and the long-handled warming pans.

The old wooden bar was set with drink mats, bowls of potato chips, and heavy ashtrays, and its polished and shiny counter attested to the many drinks that had passed over the counter top throughout the years. Spigots of draft beer and cider stood alongside the bar while bottles of spirits and a variety of soft drinks were neatly stacked in rows behind. Pewter tankards and glasses were hung in racks overhead, within easy reach of the gregarious barman. Here local politics and national problems were discussed at length in a convivial atmosphere over a pint of beer.

The pub was also the focal point for the fox hunt meets held twice a year. The meet was a splendid sight, with the pink coats of the master, huntsman, and whipper-in, the restive horses with their well-turned-out riders, and the hounds, baying eagerly, all waiting for the sound of the horn summoning them to move off.

Mr. Chamberlain, our veterinarian, lived nearby. We all knew him well, and when he asked us to look after a donkey with an injured leg, whom he wanted kept quiet, we agreed with delight. When she had recovered, I used to ride her, using binder twine as a makeshift bridle. I would climb on the fence and patiently wait until she agreed, reluctantly, to come close enough for me to climb aboard. We ambled around the fields at less than her usual speed.

All of our fields were named: one in particular was called the Banky Field, as the land was very uneven. These fields were surrounded by hedgerows, a traditional feature of the English countryside. Hedge-laying goes back seven hundred years, when it was necessary to prevent cattle from straying onto common land. It was the job of an officer, called a "hayward," to make sure the hedges were laid correctly, and a herdsman usually carried out the work of the laying.

The hedgerows were a source of great delight to me. Not only did they add to the appearance of the countryside, but they also provided food and shelter for numerous small mammals such as the shy bank mole and prickly hedgehog. Foxes made good use of the hedge to hide their dens, and even the badger, who sometimes had several entrances, dug tunnels that extended from forty to sixty feet underground. Cheeky rabbits sometimes emerged from an occupied sett, but it must have been a risky business for the rabbits, as badgers would readily eat them if given half a chance! I knew where the birds' nests were hidden and particularly loved to watch the baby birds attempting their first dangerous flight, with their mother calling frantically from a nearby branch. Often I would return home with small bunches of wildflowers for Mom, picked along these hedgerows.

Spotty, a tricolored Jack Russell, accompanied me everywhere. She had a keen nose for rabbits and often put one up while hunting along these hedgerows. The rabbit always got away after a frantic, short chase. On occasion, while sleeping by the fireside after supper, Spotty would jerk her paws and twitch her nose, making small yelping noises, dreaming of those elusive rabbits.

From a very early age, I was eager to ride anything I could-even a pig, with Dad leading it by the ear! Not as much fun as the donkey, but anything I did with my adored Dad was special for me.

Mr. Massey, a neighbor farmer friend who lived in the village, had a litter of pigs, and one was a ricklin, or runt. Much smaller than the other piglets, he was being pushed about and would have died if not taken away from his stronger brothers and sisters. When we heard about the ricklin, my brother John and I went and asked Mr. Massey if he would like to sell it and, if so, for how much. "Yes, you can have it for half a crown," he said.

We rushed home to ask Mom and Dad if we could have the money. They agreed. By this time it was getting dark, so we lit the lantern and, collecting a burlap feed sack, started back down the lane to the village to collect our little pig. We knocked on Mr. Massey's door, and when he opened it, we held up the shiny half crown.

Smiling, he came out of his house and went with us to the pigsty. The piglet squealed his objection as we picked him up and carefully wrapped him in the feed sack. Excitedly we brought him home, deciding on the way back that we would call him Fred.

On arrival at the farm, we put little Fred in a clean pigsty which we had prepared earlier with carefully shaken-out deep wheat straw. As soon as I put him on the floor, his tiny legs automatically ran to burrow in his very inviting bed.

Baby Fred, my pride and joy.

The agreement was that John would feed little Fred four times a day with a bottle and I would keep little Fred's quarters clean. However, after a few days, my brother got tired of the feeding (I think John secretly was afraid that Fred would not survive). Now Fred belonged to me.

Oh, how I loved to hold Fred in my arms and snuggle with him close to my heart and to kiss him gently on his nose. At first he would struggle and squeal and try to escape from my arms, but I would hold his little body gently but securely. Within a few days of bottle-feeding him, at the slightest sound from the sty door he would come running out of his pile of straw, eager to be fed.

Over the next few months Fred grew and developed into a beautiful pig. One morning, as we were leaning over the pigsty door, Dad came up with the idea that Fred would make a good sire to start a breeding program for purebred Landrace pigs, adding that he would love to buy him from me. Dad gave me sixteen pounds for Fred, which in those days was quite a lot of money. To my great joy, he said I now had sufficient money to buy the pony I had wanted.

In anticipation of buying a pony at the auction, we prepared the loose box, or stall. Dad and I put in three bales of wheat straw to cover the floor and with a pitchfork banked the sides of the box to make it cozy to sleep on. After we placed a flake of hay in the hay rack, everything was perfect for my new arrival.

Market day was a big event. The next local market was to be held at the Plough, a public inn, on the other side of the village at a little place called Seisdon. Advertised among the implements, cattle, sheep, and poultry was a pony, a bay gelding of twelve hands, aged eight years old. He had belonged to an old man who had recently died, and who had driven him for pleasure in a trap around the local country lanes.

It was early winter, and my Dad and I walked to the sale, my sixteen pounds hidden in my right-hand pocket with a handkerchief stuffed on top to keep them safely in place. When we arrived at the market, we were immediately surrounded by the mingled sounds of mooing cattle, the puzzled bleating of sheep, and the cackle of hens. Shrewd farmers were gathered around the pens. The auctioneer elbowed his way through the people and we heard his voice urging on the bidding. "Going . . . going . . . gone!" and another lot had been bought.

Dad and I walked toward the pen in which the pony was enclosed. I clutched his hand excitedly as we edged our way through the crowd of farmers surrounding the pony. Letting go of Dad's hand, I squeezed between the farmers and climbed up on the iron rail. Now I had a much better view, and there standing before me was the most beautiful pony I had ever seen.

My tummy was tingling with excitement as I ran my eyes over his body. He was the perfect size for me. His color was a beautiful dark bay, and he had a long tangled mane and tail with an aristocratic head and kind eyes. He was the perfect pony for me.

I glanced around at the other farmers. From their facial expressions, they looked very interested in the pony; perhaps they wanted him for their own child. My heart sank for a second. When I looked up into my Dad's face, it had a look of determination, as if he knew what was on my mind. His face broke into a smile and he said, "Pam, what do you think of him?" I could hardly contain myself with excitement, and answered, "Daddy, I love him so much, he is just the pony I have been dreaming about, please buy him for me."

Helping me down off the rail, Dad gave me a secret wink of his eye as we walked hand in hand to look over some of the other animals for sale.

When the auctioneer at last arrived by the pony, held firmly by the stockman, we were there waiting to bid. My mouth was dry, and I could hardly breathe. The bidding started, and my hands were clammy as I held them tightly together. The bidding was going along very briskly. Several farmers were bidding on my pony, until the very end, when it came down to between my Dad and an older gentleman I thought to be a grandfather.

I looked up to see my Dad nod slightly towards the auctioneer.

"Thirteen guineas I have, do I hear fourteen? Thirteen, thirteen, thirteen."

The auctioneer turned his head in the direction of the elderly man. "Do I hear fourteen?"

The man hesitantly nodded his head.

"Fourteen I have. Fourteen, fourteen, fourteen. Do I hear fifteen?"

As the auctioneer looked our way, my father gave a very confident nod.

"Fifteen I now have, fifteen, fifteen, fifteen. Do I hear sixteen?" as he looked over once more to the older gentleman.

Looking down and shaking his head, the man sadly turned away.

"If I don't hear any more bids," the auctioneer said, "this beautiful pony will be sold to the gentleman in the grey coat and his little girl. . . Going, going, gone!" he said, as his cane came down on the iron fence.

Tears ran down my cheeks as I jumped in my Dad's arms, then ran into the pen and flung my arms around my pony's neck as he was being led out of the pen and handed over to my Dad.

We were able to lead the pony home, as he was such a gentle animal. I patted him on his neck and told him how I loved him as we chatted happily on our way home along the quiet country lane. I was eight years old, the same age as my pony, and the world was truly an exciting place.

We got home just as the sun went down. After settling my pony comfortably for the night, and nearly falling asleep over supper, I tumbled into bed, to dream of flying hooves and a flowing mane as the pony and I galloped over the fields together.

Chapter 2

My First Gymkhana

The day after we brought the pony home to the farm, I awoke as the birds were just beginning to stir and dawn had barely arrived. Quickly I scrambled into my clothes and rushed out of the house. The loose boxes were only a short distance away, and as I approached them, my pony put his head over his loose box door, nickering. I slid the bolt open and slipped inside to hug him around the neck. I had decided overnight to call him Gallant Lad.

School began at nine o'clock, so I quickly fed the pony and cleaned his box. While I gave him a gentle brushing, I told him that I loved him and would see him after school, adding that Dad would let him out into his field later in the morning.

Over the next few months I rode Gallant Lad every day after school and each weekend. Initially Dad bought me only a bridle with a snaffle bit. The bridle was made of the best leather available and stitched locally. Dad told me that he would not give me a saddle for at least six months; he wanted me to ride bareback to acquire a more balanced and secure seat.

With Dad's help and advice, Gallant Lad-or Laddie, as we called him for short-and I learned how to get along together. Dad taught me how to hold the reins properly and to move my hands independently of my body while keeping my wrists supple. I learned how to guide Laddie with my legs and how to use the snaffle, keeping a gentle contact with his mouth. Fortunately Laddie had been well trained and had a light mouth.

After a while I was able to guide him wherever I wished him to go, and Dad could concentrate on teaching me how to sit properly for both the sitting and the rising trot. I found the trot tiring to begin with, but oh! it was all such fun. Cantering was much easier and I delighted in the feel of Laddie's movements beneath me.

My sisters watched my progress with interest. One day Audrey asked if she could have a ride with me. What a super idea! I thought. She scrambled up behind me and we had a wonderful time careening up and down the Banky Field, until I turned Laddie too sharply to the left, completely forgetting Audrey was a novice! Audrey fell off, pulling me with her, and we both landed in a heap on the grass. I jumped up immediately, but Audrey did not move. I can still see her now, lying there motionless. I leaned over her. "Are you dead?" I asked tremulously. Her eyes opened and she started to laugh. "No, I'm not," she replied, "but my bottom hurts a bit!" This was the first of many precarious bareback rides we shared together.

After my six months of required bareback riding, Dad told me that we were going to drive to Walsall to buy a saddle.

The town of Walsall was famous for leather goods, specializing in well-made tack. The following Saturday, after breakfast, we drove to town. After parking in the nearby car park, we entered the saddlery shop. Immediately I was overwhelmed with the aroma of new leather, which had been made into saddles, bridles, girths, and all the horse equipment a horse person would want to buy. It was displayed hanging on the walls and in the cabinets. Ladies' handbags were also sold, all of them handmade right there in a room behind the shop, which was owned and run by a husband-and-wife team, Mr. and Mrs. Young.

The bits and stirrup irons were made of stainless steel manufactured in Sheffield, a neighboring town. Exquisitely made china horses and dogs were placed neatly on shelves, but obviously out of reach of small hands like my own. I took a deep breath, savoring the moment.

After careful examination, we decided on the right saddle, together with a leather girth and a sheared sheepskin "numnah," or saddle pad. Our choice was a 15-inch Lovatt-Rickets, which had a deep seat with knee rolls and would keep me more secure on my pony. Dad and I then returned home to make sure that the saddle was a good fit for Laddie. He seemed to be very pleased with it, standing very still while Dad placed it on his back and fastened the girth to try it out. It fit him perfectly.

By now it was time for lunch. I hurried with my cottage pie, then had to wait impatiently while the rest of the family finished. At last, after helping my mother to clear away the table and wash the dishes, Dad and I walked out to Laddie's field and led him into his box. We currycombed and brushed him and then tacked him up. Dad adjusted the stirrup leathers for me and I was all set. Now I was ready to learn how to ride with a saddle.

In late spring Dad asked me if I would like to ride in two weeks' time in the local Horse Show and Gymkhana being held at Danescourt, a small village about five miles away. Would I just! Dad decided that Laddie and I should enter two events, the Apple and Bucket Race and Musical Chairs. Then I was to watch riders in other events and learn from them. I did not have proper riding attire, and it was decided that rectifying this situation was Mom's department. Luckily there was an excellent riding outfitter in the nearby town.

Two days later we went shopping. First came the boots. After trying on a number of them, I eventually decided on a dark brown pair. "But you must see that they are kept well polished," Mom told me. Next I chose fawn jodhpurs, a tie, and a well-cut tweed jacket. Finally I picked out a black velvet riding hat. I watched intently as the shopkeeper folded our purchases carefully and put them in a large brown paper bag, which I proudly carried home.

You can imagine how excited I became the closer the day of the show came. When it arrived, I got up very early in the morning, washed, dressed in my new riding attire, hurriedly ate my breakfast, and went outside to fetch Laddie from out of the field.

After he was settled in his loose box, Dad and I started to currycomb him to loosen any dirt and hair, then followed up by whisking him with a dandy brush until his coat shone like spun gold. We combed his beautiful mane and tail to perfection, and even his feet were painted with oil to make them look black and clean.

As a final touch, Dad poured a little kerosene on a cotton cloth and gently wiped it all over Laddie's back. I stared in amazement at the obviously improved shine. With a twinkle in his eye, Dad said, "That's an old farmer's secret."

Smiling, I turned and walked into the tack room to get my clean tack and, with Dad's help, saddled and bridled Laddie, double-checking to make sure everything was fitted properly.

Laddie was all ready for our wonderful day together, as Dad led him out of his box. I slipped off my overalls from over my new outfit and adjusted my hard hat. Mom and Dad waved me off, saying they would see me later at the show.

Walking through the gates of the show, Laddie pricked his ears forward, and I could feel the quiver of his body beneath me as he pranced gaily along. I leaned slightly forward and patted him on the neck. The feeling of excitement for us both was tremendous as we headed toward the secretary's tent to sign in and get our number, which was 22. I fastened it proudly around my waist.

My first class was the Apple and Bucket Race. We rode in heats, and the object of the game was to race as fast as your pony could carry you toward a bucket of water at the end of the field. You then dismounted and tried to get an apple out of the bucket with your mouth-no hands. When you had the apple between your teeth, you quickly jumped back onto your pony and galloped back to the finish line. Fortunately we were allowed to take off our coats and ties for this event!

For my next event, Musical Chairs, you and your pony galloped around a large circle of chairs, usually to the music of "Post Horn Gallop." When the music stopped, you pulled in your pony, sliding off quickly and claiming a chair. If you succeeded in getting a chair, you then remounted when the music started again.

After my events, I found a friend to look after Laddie while I wandered around, intent on taking in all the show had to offer. Local people from miles around attended these shows. The food stands sold delicious sandwiches, cakes, and lemon or orange squash. The children especially liked all the various types of ice cream that were sold. The highly competitive and colorful flower and vegetable classes were entered by most of the local farmers and gardeners.

I watched other horse classes, including the Handy Hunter Classes and the Jumping Classes. I especially enjoyed the Hackney Pony Classes, admiring the highly polished carriages, each with a well-turned-out pony and an immaculately dressed driver wearing a bowler hat and always with a blanket over his knees.

Over the next few years Laddie and I went to many shows. As we both gained more experience, we began to win prizes in the gymkhanas and our names and photographs appeared in the local newspapers. Both my parents took a great interest in my riding and accompanied me to the many horse shows I attended. They were always very supportive and never

Riding Gallant Lad at my first horse show,
chatting with Lord Dartmouth and Mr. Butler.
I would have died of embarrassment if I had known there
were flys on Laddie's face and that his noseband wasn't straight.

made me feel they were disappointed when I did not win a ribbon, as some parents did with their children.

Eventually I grew too big for my darling Laddie, and Dad decided that we would have to look for a larger pony. I knew he was right, but I agreed with him only on the condition that we found an excellent local home for Laddie. We were fortunate. The parents of a girl who had been one of my competitors asked if I would consider selling Laddie for their younger daughter. I knew that Laddie would be going to a good home, so we said, "Yes, but could you please wait for a month?" I could not bear the thought of Laddie going straight away.

A month later, the young girl came with her parents to collect Laddie in their horse trailer, and I felt better when I saw how thrilled she was, throwing her arms around Laddie's neck and kissing him. As they drove away, my last sight of Laddie that day, through tear-misted eyes, was the top of his green rug and his tail hanging over the back of the horse trailer door. I consoled myself with the thought that I would still be seeing him at the shows.

Bandit was the horse Dad found for me. He belonged to a horse dealer Dad had known for years, an honest man whose son had outgrown Bandit and was now riding in the adult classes. My new horse was a ten-year-old, 14.2-hands, liver chestnut gelding with a white star on his forehead, and very handsome he was. Under Dad's supervision I now started show jumping and fox hunting. Bandit was an experienced horse, and over the next few years we were to be seen at the local horse shows and out hunting with the local hunt. I particularly loved fox hunting and cubbing, getting up at three o'clock and then, after the hunt, hacking back home sometimes as far as ten miles. Bandit and I would return home weary but very happy, with Bandit looking forward to his warm box and food manger and I to our warm kitchen and a hot bath.

Myself as a teenager on Bandit with Spotty I.

(24)

Chapter 3

The Riding School

Now I had arrived at the great age of sixteen! This was the legal age to leave high school, and I was to continue my education part-time at an agricultural college nearby, giving me a little more time with my pony.

To my great delight, Dad agreed that now might be the time for us to embark on a wonderful adventure! We decided to buy some young horses, break them in ourselves, and later open a riding school.

About thirty miles away from the farm there was an area in Shropshire called the Clee hills. This spectacular countryside of hills and dales of green grass, reeds, bracken, and the purple hue of rough heather was laced with clear, sparkling streams trickling over pebbly beds. There was a marvelous feeling of freedom here; you felt you could stretch your arms and fly when you stood on a hill and were able to see for miles over the countryside. The land here was "common land," which meant that anyone who lived on the Clee was allowed to graze their animals free.

The farmers' cottages were small, with low-beam ceilings and large fireplaces to burn peat, which was on their own land and cut out of the ground when needed. Sometimes a fallen tree also gave them some wood. The cottages were whitewashed with lime and water.

Their lives were hard, and they basically lived from hand to mouth. Rearing the ponies, cattle, and sheep on the hills provided their only income, as there was not any other way of life except for farming.

No one had a telephone, so when Mom, Dad, and I were making plans to drive the thirty miles hoping to buy ponies, we would ring the post office on the hills, and they would be kind enough to give the farmer our message.

Over the next several years Mom, Dad, and I made good friends with several of these farmers. They sold us a considerable number of free-roaming ponies of all sizes and colors. The farmer would round up the wild ponies before we arrived, putting them in an enclosed area.

The horse trailer was backed into position by the enclosure. As we neared the ponies they pushed and shoved and tried to clamber over each other, not knowing what to do. They whinnied and snorted and showed the whites of their eyes in fright. Little did they know some of them were headed for a far better way of life.

Leaning over the fence looking at ponies was always a thrill. Trying to choose the right one was difficult, as none of them would stand still a second for us to look at their legs and feet to see if they were sound. So Dad and I really chose them by their color, height, and condition. There was no way we could decide on their temperament, because at that time they were all highly strung.

After we made our choices, the gate was half opened, allowing the others to run out over the hills, kicking up their heels in relief. Ponies in the wild always have a leader, so my father would borrow an old quiet pony named Jeb from a neighbor to take with us as a babysitter for the three-year-olds. Jeb was standing quietly at the bottom of the ramp, which had high gates on either side as extra protection for the ponies. The three ponies we had chosen were herded close to Jeb who, with his experience, knew what was expected of him. He walked gently up the ramp leading the three ponies behind him.

Once all four were boarded, Dad, the farmer, and I quickly lifted the ramp into position on the horse trailer, closing it securely. After bargaining amicably over the price and concluding our business, we were usually invited in by the farmer for a welcome cup of tea. Driving back home, we always took great care not to sway the trailer any more than necessary, to prevent the ponies from falling and hurting themselves.

The ponies we broke were usually over three years old and each pony had a different personality. Our first pony had a mind of his own, with a look in his eyes as wild as the wind blowing over the Clee hills on a cold, grey winter's day. All his short life he had been running free over the hills, untouched by human hand-and he intended to stay that way!

I did not try to force him. I had prepared his loose box with sweet-smelling hay and placed grain in his manger. That first day he just stood in the far corner of his loose box, snorting fearfully and showing the whites of his eyes. I spoke quietly to him, saying, "Settle down, lad, you are going to be just fine." I then turned and walked out of the loose box, securely fastening the bolt on the door.

Gradually over the next few days he settled down and began to look forward to my arrival with his food. I was able to stroke his face and pat his neck, all the time speaking to him in a soothing tone of voice. He eventually trusted me sufficiently to allow me to brush his body and legs, even permitting me to pick dirt out of his feet. He began to enjoy the attention.

The next step was to put a leather halter on his head to enable me to lead him. I held the halter in my left hand and slowly put my right hand over his neck, at the same time lifting the halter in place over his nose and resting the headpiece behind his ears.

As I was slipping the halter over his ears, he lifted his head a little higher, trying to get out of my reach. Stretching my body and standing on tiptoes, I eased the halter over into position. Once the halter was in place, he lowered his head.

Tom, a young fair-haired lad who worked on the farm, had a way with horses. He was waiting to help me as I led the pony by the lead rein out of his loose box. The pony stopped abruptly as we emerged into the yard, standing with all four feet planted firmly on the ground. Tom walked to his hindquarters and patted him on his flanks to encourage him to walk forward. The next second the pony reared up, then lunged forward with me hanging onto the lead for dear life.

I quickly gathered myself together and held onto his halter, digging my heels into the ground for more strength. Again, he lunged forward, dragging me with him. His head was held high, and with the power of his flexed muscles he tried to shake me loose. I held on tightly, leaning my shoulder against his as a support to enable me to hang on. We were heading toward a wall several yards away. I envisioned us both smashing into it and collapsing in a heap on the ground.

But I managed to gather up more strength in my hands and arms and to bring him to a standstill before we had a collision. We were both out of breath and shaking a little. He turned his head towards me, ears pricked forward, as if to say, "Huh, I'm not too sure about this." I patted him, saying, "Good boy, that wasn't so bad, was it?" I walked him around the yard a few times, then gave him a carrot as a reward, and returned him to his loose box. Enough for one day.

Over the next few days of careful handling, he soon became used to being led around and to trust us. He accepted the bridle and snaffle bit and was now ready for the big step of putting the saddle across his back and gradually fastening the girth. This can be a frightening experience for a pony, but with patience and gentle words he accepted the saddle without protest.

Then, as I gathered both reins in my hand, Tom gave me a leg up and I carefully sat astride the pony, sitting still for a moment, talking and patting his neck. When asked to walk forward with Tom leading him around the box, the pony hunched his back. I thought he was going to buck, but he relaxed his body, and Tom led him out into the yard as I guided him gently but firmly with my hands on the reins and pressure from my legs.

This procedure was followed for breaking all the ponies and horses that came to Springhill Farm. With some of the stronger, bigger horses, I would longe them first (to longe, you fasten a long rein to the halter and stand in the center with your horse trotting or cantering around you in a circle). This helped release some of their energy before we attempted to saddle up and ride.

Within less than a year, our riding school grew into a thriving business. Initially Dad helped me build a good-size riding ring, and later we made six assorted jumps. With lessons I learned from Dad, I gradually taught more and more young riders. I found I could teach! Word spread locally, and before too long I had as many students as I could manage.

My first student, Brian, was a timid, small, slender eight-year-old lad who lived in a town and had never been around any animals at all. His mother had taught me at school when I was six. I expected him to be afraid of the horses, but to my surprise, his reaction was quite the opposite.

I introduced Brian to Gypsy, a gentle, 12.2-hand grey mare, and gave him a few pointers. I told him always to say hello and give his mount a pat on the neck or stroke the nose before mounting. A good way to make friends with your mount, I said, was to offer a carrot, and often the next time you had a riding lesson you would be greeted with a whinny, which always gives you a special feeling. At Brian's first lesson on the lead line, he was taught how to hold his reins, how to sit, and how to put his feet in the stirrups. I then mounted Bandit, and we headed for the riding ring. Brian was a good student, eager to learn, and before long he was able to ride on his own.

Any new student would be asked whether they knew how to ride. "Oh, yes," some would reply. "How many times have you ridden?" I would inquire. "I've never been on a horse, but I have watched them on television!" I smiled to myself at their unknowing words. It is one thing to watch someone else ride, but it's up a different street actually to put it into motion yourself. As soon as a student mounted a horse, I usually got a pretty good idea if he or she was going to be a good rider. Some students, however hard as they tried, would never be any better than an average rider. It is a talent that you are born with and has a lot to do with coordination.

Each pony had a different temperament. Some were highly strung and full of energy, while others could be rather lazy and laid back. It is that kind you have to be careful of; if they think you have let your guard down, they are apt to give a buck or even rear in the air and wheel around. I found every pony a big challenge.

Running the riding school of thirty horses and ponies was a great responsibility for me, and I put in long, hard-working hours. I was constantly worrying that one of my students would fall and get hurt. One case in particular comes to mind. I was out riding cross country with six students. It was a glorious day, and we were all greatly enjoying the ride. Suddenly, for no apparent reason, Sandy, a usually quiet,

16.2-hand chestnut gelding, bolted with his fairly experienced middle-aged rider, Doris. At the time, we were riding at the edge of a ploughed field, and Sandy went off at a full gallop over the deep furrows. Doris was frantically pulling on both reins, which had no effect whatsoever on the horse. She was panicking and obviously getting very tired.

Riding a bolting horse can be a very frightening experience. I turned to the other riders and asked them to please stand still and wait while I helped Doris handle her horse. I did not want them galloping after Doris, as it would have made Sandy run faster. I shouted to Doris to turn her horse to the left and try to keep him going in a full circle-hoping that Sandy would tire galloping over the deeply ploughed field. Doris's face by this time was very pale, and she looked frightened, but she gamely hung on, listening to my instructions as I shouted again to keep pulling the rein to the left as hard as she could. Gradually the big chestnut did turn and begin to tire and slow down, sweating and breathing heavily, and finally came to a standstill. Trembling and exhausted, Doris turned toward me and said with a brave, slightly shaky smile, "Well, I certainly learned a good lesson today!"

Besides buying and breaking ponies and horses for my riding school, and running the school itself, I also trained horses for shows and to be ridden out fox hunting. I was also breeding Scotch collies, which were a very popular breed at that time. I never understood why none of my brothers or sisters had shown any interest in either the horses or the dogs at home. At any rate, by the time I was fifteen years old, they were all married and had

*Just William and I
before the meet with the Albrighton hounds,
which met at the Greyhound.*

left home, and I was the only remaining member of the family living with Dad and Mom.

Everything in my life seemed to be going perfectly. I was happy and busy. I was attending a nearby agricultural day college and had recently joined the Young Farmers' Club at Kidderminster in Worcestershire. This club had a large membership of two hundred young adults between the ages of twenty and thirty. The main meeting was held once a month for a learning program, but every week we would get together for various social outings, which were always a lot of fun.

At my first club meeting I was nervous. It was a talk on dairy cows, a very popular program that was well attended by both young men and young women, offspring of the area farmers. Following the program, everyone gathered in groups talking to each other. As I was being introduced around, standing before me, seemingly from out of nowhere, was a very attractive man with a smile on his face from ear to ear. He seemed a little cheeky, as he had edged his way through the other young farmers, and he introduced himself as Peter.

The meeting had come to an end, and several of the members were going to a cafe for a cup of coffee. Peter invited me along and, since we both had cars, I was to follow him, driving my car. When I entered the cafe, a four-seat booth was nearest to me, and as I sat down, Peter quickly slipped in and sat beside me. As we chatted over our coffee, he seemed so full of life and self-confidence.

Our conversation went on as if I had known him a long time. He was so easy to talk to. His mother had been a widow since he was a little boy, and he had one brother, John, who was two years younger and also a member of the club. I listened to him with interest and studied his face as he talked. He had dark brown hair, a part on the left side, cut short on the back and sides. His ears were kind of large and bent forward a little. His nose was an average shape but had a small scar on the bridge, as if he had been kicked by a cow. It looked very similar to a scar on my brother John's nose, from being kicked by a young heifer the first time she was being milked. Peter's eyes were brown and twinkling. His jaw was strong and square, while his cheekbones were high, and his complexion was ruddy and healthy-looking. He was obviously an outdoor man. He was six feet tall and, under his brown sport coat and grey flannel trousers, he looked to be lean and strong and agile.

He went on to tell me he had been granted a loan from the government to build a huge greenhouse, enabling him to grow more tomatoes and cucumbers on his small holding.

The evening came to an end all too soon, and Peter asked if he could see me the next evening. My heart skipped a beat as I accepted his invitation.

On our first date, Peter collected me in his red Mini car to take me to a Young Farmers' dance in Bridgenorth, a very old town built up on a hill overlooking the River Severn. Peter arrived at our farm promptly at seven o'clock that Saturday evening and I introduced him to my parents. I could see that they took to him immediately. On the way to the dance we chatted and discovered how much we had in common. We both loved horses, dogs, dancing, and swimming, and enjoyed farming. Arriving at the pub, the Rose and Crown, we found the dance was in full swing. What a wonderful evening we had together. Over the next year we saw each other often.

To make me independent, my parents gave me one of their remodeled farm workers' cottages. The two-bedroom cottage was built of brick, with a slate-tiled roof, enclosed by a four-foot brick wall. There was a small garden in both the front and the back. The front gate opened onto a path leading up to the front door through a mass of flowers and shrubs. Red and pink roses intertwined with honeysuckle grew on either side of the porch, flowering profusely with a delightful scent during spring and summer. The front door had a well-polished brass-cow door knocker and a letter box.

One cold and frosty Saturday morning in December I was returning home from a hunt meet at the nearby Claverly village. I was driving my car at a normal speed when I came over a small rise in the road. Suddenly I hit some black ice, which I never saw. The car slid into the hedge at the side of the road, bounced over to the other side, and turned over twice. I was thrown out of the door and landed on the road on my back.

Within moments people were there to help. An ambulance arrived, and I was gently lifted onto a stretcher and driven to the nearby hospital. I went in and out of consciousness and was only vaguely aware of what was happening. Much later, when I awoke in the hospital, my head was bandaged and I had twenty stitches. My whole body was in a plaster cast. I had broken my back. My family was gathered anxiously around me, looking very concerned, and my parents looked extremely grave.

My world had shattered. I was in the hospital for two weeks. When my doctor told me that I could go home, my parents came and collected me from the hospital and took me back home to Springhill Farm. Their love and concern helped me recover from my injury. My brothers and sisters also rallied round and gave me every encouragement and support. I will always be grateful for the love and comfort of my family during this time. Thanks in large part to their help, the pain began to recede little by little as the months went by.

My head wounds healed well, but it was my injured lower back that continued to cause me pain and a slow recovery. I had broken one of my vertebrae and for the next four months had to continue to wear the body cast. Later I was given a brace to support my back in place of the body cast. I had to endure the cast for many more months while at the same time undergoing regular heat treatment and physiotherapy. It was a long uphill struggle, but gradually I began to recover and was able to do some light work about the farm.

But my whole world-including the thriving riding school-had crashed on that cold and frosty December morning.

Chapter 4

My Father's Farm

A year had gone by since the accident, and I was now twenty-four years old. It was a late spring afternoon, and I was in the lounge with my parents enjoying a cup of tea after a busy day on the farm. We sat chatting quietly by the leaded bay window, watching the sun going down and the shadows lengthening in the nearby fields. The window was open, and during a lull in the conversation we could hear the birds chirping sleepily, settling down for the night. I felt more relaxed and content than I had at any time since the accident. I think my parents realized this because, with unspoken agreement, they broached their ideas of changing things on the farm, which they had discussed together during the past few months.

As my riding career was over, Dad suggested that we open a boarding kennel. There were no kennels in the area, and he believed that there was a definite need for one. I was immediately enthusiastic, knowing how the English, like myself, love their dogs, often quite as much as their own children!

Spotty, the Jack Russell, was my special dog when I was a little girl. Jack Russells are terrier-type dogs which most farmers like to have around the farm buildings to keep the rats and mice at bay. Spotty was given to me by my brother. She was my first dog, and I never trained her. She was my little pet, and used to follow when I was riding my pony. She naturally behaved herself, never saw a lead, never had a collar on her neck, and came immediately when called. That was the social pattern of dogs on the farm.

Black and white Welsh collie dogs play a major role in farm living. They are able to do the work of six people, herding the cattle, sheep, and even pigs, enabling one person to handle many animals. This saves a lot of legwork when moving livestock from field to field or corralling them in enclosures to make it easy to worm the animals or shear sheep in the spring.

Lassie was one of my heroes as a teenager, and it was quite easy to persuade my parents to buy male and female Scotch collies from two different litters and start a small breeding program. Somehow, over the years, two collies became six, mainly because we loved them so much that it was difficult to sell them as puppies.

I learned from my Dad how to choose the right sire for the puppies, so as to breed a collie not only to be beautiful but also to have an even temperament to sell as a house pet or as a quick-minded working dog on a farm. My father also taught me how to groom, bathe, and train the dogs; he in turn had been taught by his father, a red-bearded Scotsman who died when I was two years old.

At the beginning of the week after our decision to open a kennel, I drove into Seisdon to get a license for the boarding kennels, and it was given to me that same day. I drove home triumphantly.

Our plans included kennels for two hundred dogs. The plans were passed the following week by the county planning board, so now it was full steam ahead!

A distance from the house was a large brick building with spacious windows, two large doors, and a tiled roof. The building had never been put to full use, and Dad thought it would be the most convenient for a kennel and would not be too great an expense to modernize.

The floor was dirt, which made it easy to prepare for the concrete, laid with a slight slant toward a channel so the water would drain. There were kennels on either side of the building with a walkway down the center aisle. The large windows gave a bright and airy look to the place.

A wall twelve feet from the end was the divider for the office, with a double glass door making easy access into the kennels-large and spacious for the dogs, slightly smaller for the cats, each with its own cozy bed. Overhanging shades were intermittent and had low-voltage bulbs so the light would not be too bright. Heating came from blowers at each end of the building to create a comfortable controlled temperature.

Completion of the kennels and cattery took just over three months. We hung baskets of flowers outside the office, and at intervals through the runs. Everything looked spick-and-span, and we were ready for the grand opening. Our first advertisement in the local newspaper, the *Express and Star*, read quite simply: "Springhill Farm is proud to announce the opening of a Boarding and Training Kennel. Every attention given to your pets. Contact Pam Dickson. Telephone 37734."

The response from the Wolverhampton area was overwhelming. We were soon busy coping with the day-to-day running of a busy kennel. Mom was the secretary, and she ran an efficient office. I was in charge of the administration of the kennels, overseeing kennel maids who helped with cleaning the kennels and feeding, grooming, clipping, bathing, and exercising the dogs and cats.

The most common breeds that stayed at our kennel were corgis, German shepherds (called Alsatians in England), Labradors, and poodles. Many of our clients boarded their dogs with us during the holidays, collecting them on Sunday evening. That made Sunday a busy, hectic time. Mom would prepare the bills while the kennel maids and I got the dogs ready for the owners.

To keep up with the arriving clients, I would greet them as they drove up, walk sedately into the kennels, and, as soon as I rounded the corner, dash off to get their dog, brushed and readied earlier, and bring it out to a happy, beaming owner. The dogs were as excited as their owners, and with much tail wagging and woofs would leap into their car, barking their happiness to be back with their master or mistress.

The hustle and bustle of dogs departing taught me one lesson in kennel management the hard way. It was surprising how often clients with names such as Jones, Smith, Brown, or

Green happened to own dogs with names like Jack, Sam, Rebel, or Patch. One afternoon, Mrs. Jones, a sophisticated, elegantly attired elderly woman, arrived to pick up her corgi, Jack. It so happened that we had boarding with us a number of male corgis, all named Jack, and all very similar in appearance.

I brought one of the Jacks out to her, but there was no recognition on either side. Stiffly she said, "That is not my dog." "Oh dear, I am so sorry, Mrs. Jones," I replied, quickly backing off and escaping with the offending Jack. Hastily trying to rectify my error, I presented her with another Jack. To my dismay, I had the wrong Jack again! This time Mrs. Jones was very angry and upset indeed. Again I apologized profusely.

By now I was equally upset and extremely flustered but managed to keep a calm exterior. I returned yet again to the kennels and collected still another Jack.

Phew! When I appeared, this little Jack saw his mistress and barked excitedly, tugging on the lead. To my vast relief, this produced an immediate and remarkable transformation in Mrs. Jones. Her anger dissolved and her eyes lit up with joy. She scooped this third Jack into her arms and murmured to him, "This is my boy, good boy, Jack."

Mrs. Jones forgave me and recommended our kennels to her friends. A muddle never happened again! I had learned my lesson, and after this episode we were very careful to ensure that we placed a card on each dog's kennel door bearing its name and the name and address of the owner.

I was naturally taught that to get a person or an animal to respond, you have to be kind. You've got to gain their respect.

Dogs basically have the same mental and physical quirks as people, and you can't handle one dog the same way as another. Dogs have their own personalities-some timid, some aggressive, while others are relaxed and nothing seems to upset them. With patience and understanding, a dog can be taught almost anything and can become a real member of the family.

To have a highly trained dog, you need to get it young, about six weeks old. Then you have a chance of anticipating its movements and emotions. Six weeks to six months is the most crucial part of a puppy's life; it determines how the rest of its life is going to turn out. It's important for a puppy to have a lot of handling and deep, loving affection, and to be told how good it is. To touch a puppy all over, from the head to the tail, is important. For example, if a child pulls a dog's tail or ear, its instinct is to turn quickly and see what is happening. But with earlier handling, the dog takes it in stride.

Once a dog has been trained, it will rarely forget. To give you an example, a few months after we opened the kennels there were stories in the paper about a white German shepherd that had been seen by farmers roaming over the fields. For several months it had been killing chickens, and a reward was out for shooting it, but it couldn't be caught. Our farmhouse was on the top of a hill, and you could see for miles from the window. If anybody was working in the fields, we would hang a towel out of the window at lunchtime, and from a long distance they could see that lunch was ready.

I was up in the bathroom one day, looking out the window, and saw a white object over in the Cumberland Field.

It turned out to be the shepherd. After that, we took particular note of it. Our next door neighbor had a lot of chickens in the field, and the little henhouses were dotted all over, so we took turns watching the dog.

One time, while I was watching, the dog began to creep along on its stomach, slouched, all the way down the Banky Field and another field, looking toward where the chickens were. You could imagine what was going through its mind. It crawled quietly, hesitating so the chickens didn't know it was there. All of a sudden, with a quick dash, it ran to the nearest chicken, picked it up in its mouth, and ran to the Cumberland Field, where it lay down and ate the bird.

It wasn't as if the dog ran into the chickens, biting at them and killing them all as a fox would do. It chose only one chicken, so we didn't say a word to anyone. The dog was obviously getting the food it needed to survive. This went on for a couple of weeks. It was incredible to watch the way the shepherd worked. It was cunning and knew exactly what it was doing. After eating it would lie at the top of the hill relaxing in the sun.

There was a boy who worked for us named Michael, whose great pride, even in those days, was going to the hairdresser and getting his hair shampooed. He was going down to the Cumberland Field to get the cows to go in for milking, when he saw the white dog go into an oak tree stump, which was hollow at the bottom. He was near enough to tell she was nursing puppies. You couldn't usually get close to the dog, but this day Michael did.

I knew she had to be captured to prevent her being shot, and to keep the puppies from growing up wild. With Michael I got a collar and lead, and took a noose with me. The dog sat still, just behind the little entrance into the stump. It was a perfect home for her babies. There were six puppies about five weeks old, all big and fat. I didn't want to put my hand in. I knew the dog had been somebody's pet, but she'd been on her own for quite a few months. I decided to make my movements slow and easy and talk softly, to comfort her.

She didn't growl or show hostility when I bent down, but I couldn't take the chance of slipping my hand in. I put the noose at the end of a long stick, slipped it over her head, and gently began to pull her. She began to fight a little, trying to shake the noose from around her neck, then sat up on her haunches, planting her feet firmly on the rotted mulch at the base of the hollow tree. I coaxed her to the entrance, and was pulling her out. That was when she bit me.

Despite being bitten, I persisted. Once she was outside the stump, I slipped the collar over her head. I didn't want to take the chance of her getting away, because I thought a mean person might shoot her for the reward. I loosened the noose, at the same time putting the collar attached to the leash around her neck. When I took the noose off, she began to relax.

While walking back home, I was surprised at how well she led. Michael carried all six puppies in his arms. We put her in the stable with her puppies. To prevent people from trying to track her, we called the police to tell them we had captured the dog.

My parents had to sign a form saying we'd be held responsible for any damage the dog might do. Luckily, she turned out to be a beautiful dog. The puppies were gorgeous and healthy, and when they were old enough, we gave them away to local people.

We named her Lucy, and she wasn't a wild dog; she was a very kind dog. We were always afraid to let her loose, on the off chance she'd leave the farm. Eventually we found the perfect home for her, with a woman who lived far away from our neighbors' chickens. Lucy quickly acclimatized herself to a wonderful new way of life. I missed her dearly, but under the circumstances we had made the right decision.

Our farm truly had become a busy, thriving place. In addition to our boarding and training kennels, we expanded our dairy farm operations. We decided to replace the Friesian herd we owned with Jersey cows, while at the same time retaining our herd of black Aberdeen Angus steers. Jerseys need less acreage to graze and don't eat as many meal pellets as Friesians. The Jersey cow is a much smaller, lighter-boned animal, lovely creamy brown in color with a dishlike face and large, kind eyes. Their milk is rich and creamy.

Gradually we built up a good herd of Jersey cattle. We bought a number of our Jersey cows in Utoxeter in Hertfordshire, about sixty miles away. We also bought young heifers in calf from neighboring farms, building up a select Jersey herd. Our cow sheds were repainted inside and out, and we even decorated the sheds with hanging baskets of flowers, just as we had done with the kennels.

Morning and evening, the cows were milked to music from a radio, playing jazz or classical music. I know the cows enjoyed the music while munching on their morning and evening meal, as they often switched their tails gently to and fro as if keeping time with the music.

We even used to groom the cattle. They'd lie down in a mess, so we groomed them as if they were horses, until they were sleek. Grooming made them quieter and was good for the hygiene of the milk. If the milk was cleaner, you'd get a penny a gallon more. We'd wash the udder before milking, so no dirt would go into the milk from the teat. The milk was collected daily by the Midlands County Dairy, a short distance away.

The kennels and our cattle herds were keeping both Dad and me very busy. Thanks to all the hard work, I was now leading a full and active life. I had little time to be depressed, and I began to resume my social life. I rejoined the Young Farmers' Club and went dancing and ice skating. My back had healed well, although it has always given me trouble from time to time whenever I do too much.

But even as I was regaining my mental and physical well-being, a storm cloud appeared on the horizon, gradually growing larger and threatening my new-found happiness. My father's health was beginning to fail. He had to be careful not to catch cold and was often unable to leave the house, choosing rather to sit by the fireside and do the farm accounts. I now took over the management of the farm.

One Friday evening I attended a twenty-first birthday party for my friend Angela. As usual, when I returned home Dad was waiting up for me to hear all about the evening. We sat by the fireside while we talked about the party, and I was encouraged that he seemed quite like his old self. The following evening, I went out again and returned home at midnight. The same as the night before, I went straight to the sitting room. The fire had died down, with only a small flickering log left. The room felt cold. Dad was slumped in his favorite chair, his glasses lying on the floor by his feet and the newspaper crumpled on his lap. The room was strangely quiet. With a shiver of apprehension I walked slowly towards him. I knew then that he was dead. I bent over my Dad, tears flooding down my cheeks.

I crossed the room to the telephone and with trembling fingers dialed our doctor's number. Mom was asleep upstairs; I didn't go to her until after the doctor had arrived. We then went upstairs together, and he told her in his kind and forthright way. She took the news badly, and he stayed with her until the medicine he gave her calmed her down. Meanwhile I rang my sister Audrey, who lived twenty miles away, and she came immediately. Dad died on the same day as Sir Winston Churchill, January 24, 1965.

The farm was not the same after we lost Dad. He and I had always worked together in perfect harmony. Without Dad's experience, guidance, and help, I found I just could not cope on my own. There was too much to manage and too much pressure. A deep depression developed, and I suffered a nervous breakdown, ending up in the hospital.

When I recovered somewhat, I stayed with my sister Audrey and her family. My elder brother Gordon kept the farm going. When I finally returned home, I made every effort to settle down to my old life. But without Dad I found that, try as I might, I simply was unable to carry on as before. The doctor suggested I go away for a holiday. It was probably selfish of me, but I had a strong desire to escape completely from my memories. I had always wanted to go to America, so I decided that now was the time.

Chapter 5

Coming to America

By now it was the beginning of October 1965. I awoke early on the day of my departure for America, having slept badly all night. Was I really certain I wanted to go off to the States on my own, to a land where I had neither relations nor friends? I had never flown before in my life. Would I enjoy the flight or be miserable?

In the dim light I looked first at my suitcases neatly packed, placed by my bedroom door, then at the chair where I had placed my traveling clothes and handbag containing my flight ticket and traveler's checks. The door opened quietly, and Mom was standing there holding a cup of steaming tea.

I know she realized how I was feeling. She came over to my bed, placed the tea on my bedside table, then turned to go out of the room, saying, "You had better get up now, Pam darling, as we have a long drive to the airport." Her matter-of-fact and reassuring attitude was just what I needed to lay aside my misgivings, and I left my bed resolved to embark on my journey, come what may.

Mom, Audrey, and I arrived at Heathrow Airport over an hour before the late-morning scheduled departure of my flight. I stood in the queue at the British Airways counter to check in. My turn came, and I was told that my cases were overweight! In those days you were only allowed forty-four pounds weight, not including a handbag and a coat. Horrors! What a traumatic experience after my efforts to pack carefully and take only what I absolutely needed! However, very reluctantly I managed to eliminate still more of my "absolute necessities" and hurriedly repacked with Mom and Audrey's help. Rejoining the queue, I weighed in again, and this time my luggage was just under the maximum weight.

My ticket and passport were checked, and I was assigned a window seat. Nothing remained to be done except to wait for my flight to be called.

It is always difficult to chat to family or friends seeing you off on a long journey. This was the case now. Everything had been said, and I was getting nervous about the flight, though determined not to show it. At long last, my flight was called. Tears welled in our eyes as we wrapped our arms around each other, not really wanting to let go. My legs were a little weak as I pulled myself away to walk through the barrier, glancing back over my shoulder to get my last glimpse of my mother and my sister before boarding the plane.

The plane took off and, as we soared westward over England and the ocean, I discovered to my great relief that flying held no fears for me. In fact, the flight was a grand new adventure and I enjoyed every minute of it. I refused to permit my mind to dwell on the frightening aspect of arriving in an unknown country on my own.

We landed at Kennedy Airport in the late afternoon. I collected my suitcases and went through immigration and customs. I was pleasantly surprised to find how friendly and welcoming the officials were. Walking outside the airport building, I hailed a taxi, trustingly placed myself in the hands of the driver, and asked him to take me to the nearest good hotel. The driver did not have a uniform like the cabbies in England do, but he knew exactly where he was going and seemed pleased to have an English lady in his cab. He told me a couple of English jokes, which I chuckled at with delight.

It was an exciting drive. The trucks and large cars, so much bigger than in England, roared along the busy highway in the congested traffic at what appeared to me to be a terrifying speed. I was taken aback by the size of the buildings, far taller and larger than anything I had ever seen back home.

My taxi stopped by the International Hotel. My naive faith in my driver proved not to be misplaced, and I was not disappointed in his choice of hotels. At the check-in desk, there were many people from all over the world who wanted to stay the night there too!

My room was fourteen floors up, and I had an incredible view from my window. By this time it was dark, and the night sky was aglow with the glitter of a thousand lights from the city spread out before me-truly a new experience for a country girl. Something else more down to earth was also new in my experience. I tried without success to open my window to appreciate the view fully, and thus had my first encounter with the sealed windows of modern skyscrapers. I loved the view but was not particularly impressed with the window.

After ringing my family to tell them I had arrived safely, I had a warm bath, then climbed into bed exhausted by all the excitement of the day.

The next morning I awoke feeling refreshed. After dressing in slacks and a jersey, I packed my suitcases and went downstairs for breakfast. I sat at the cafe counter and ordered a full breakfast. I was hungry, not having had dinner the night before, but I did not expect the huge repast put before me: several pieces of bacon, two eggs, tomatoes, fried potatoes, and toast. To my shame, I thoroughly enjoyed every morsel.

After the excellent meal, I went over to the front desk to ask one of the clerks to recommend an honest car dealership in the vicinity. She gave me the name and address of one nearby, adding that the owner, Mr. Selcom, was one of the better people in the business.

Mr. Selcom was in the office when I arrived by taxi with all my luggage. He suggested that I put my suitcases in his secretary's office while we looked around his car lot. I explained that I wanted to buy a secondhand sports car that was in good condition, as I planned to drive across the country. "I have the perfect car for you," he told me. We walked across the lot and stopped before a beautiful 1962 red convertible MG. The car appeared to be in good condition and, after bargaining over the price, I eventually bought it for $500. I was so pleased-I could never have bought a car like that in England for that price.

After paying for my car, I stowed my suitcases in the boot and climbed into my new car with a big smile on my face. Mr. Selcom gave me a map of the States and directed me how to get out of New York City. He advised me to drive carefully and wished me a good day. I must say that I have always had a warm spot in my heart for Mr. Selcom. Not only was the price right, but he was as good as his word-my little MG performed valiantly throughout the long journey I was about to begin.

The journey, however, had a nerve-racking start. As soon as I drove out into the busy street I became nervous. Actually, it was terrifying! Here I was in New York, driving on the wrong side of the road in a stream of fast-moving traffic-horns blaring, brakes squealing, and my small MG dwarfed by the huge trucks roaring past. I was too nervous to drive fast, and my fellow drivers were soon hooting at me to get a move on. My hands were planted firmly on the steering wheel, but I had butterflies in my tummy. I could not find anywhere to stop to look at the map, so I just drove, watching for signs for Route 95 South and the New Jersey Turnpike, as Mr. Selcom had directed me.

As silly as it sounds, I gave credit to a tractor back on the farm, which I had driven in many difficult situations, for giving me the confidence to drive in New York without an incident. Eventually I found myself on the right road and drove safely away from the busy New York traffic, as I started to get the hang of driving in these strange new surroundings.

Over the next three months, I saw America as some of its residents never do. From New Jersey I drove to Pennsylvania and on to Ohio, through Indiana and Illinois. I crossed the wide Mississippi River at St. Louis and then drove along the straight highways through miles and miles of never-ending wheat fields in Kansas.

Driving over the Rocky Mountains in Colorado was a wonderful experience, but scary when the edge on one side of the winding, precarious road was a sheer drop of hundreds of feet into the valley below. From Denver and the Rockies I headed southwest to Arizona and the Grand Canyon, a spectacular wilderness of stone. Then on to Las Vegas, its glittering lights and colors a sharp contrast to the sparse, fascinating desert around it. I continued my journey west to California, which was drier and less verdant than I expected and where, in Hollywood, with my red MG, head scarf, and sunglasses, I was once mistaken by passersby for a movie star! Since I didn't have a schedule, I sometimes stayed several days in one place if it held a special interest for me.

When the time came for me to travel back to the East Coast, I chose a more southerly route, to Arizona, New Mexico, and the Texas Panhandle, on into the deep south of Louisiana, Mississippi, Alabama, and Georgia. Then I headed northeast through the Carolinas and into Washington, D.C. I arrived there three months after my odyssey across America began, and here I took a plane from Dulles Airport home to England.

My homecoming in England was short-lived. I found I was restless and unsettled and, without Dad, had lost my enthusiasm for taking care of the farm. My thoughts kept returning to America, and finally I gathered my courage and announced to my family that I was going back, this time to work. My mother was very unhappy at the thought of me living and working abroad. I explained to her that America was the land of opportunity and I would like to be given a chance to succeed on my own. I had enough money for a one-way ticket plus fifty pounds.

Chapter 6

Harness Racing

I was intrigued by the challenge of a position I had seen advertised in an American magazine, *The Harness Horse*. The advertisement was placed by a Mr. Del Miller, a well-known person in harness-racing circles and the owner of the Meadowlands, a racetrack in Pennsylvania.

Mr. Miller was looking for someone to work with his trotters and pacers. Such an opportunity would present a brand new and challenging experience for me. The more I considered the idea, the more I became convinced this was for me, so I applied for the position, and was hired, sight unseen.

After landing at Dulles Airport near Washington, D.C., I caught a Greyhound bus to Pittsburgh. Stepping off the bus, clutching my case and feeling quite a bit insecure, I glanced nervously around looking for the man who was supposed to meet me but whom I had never seen. The bus depot was crowded and noisy, jammed with all kinds of people, seemingly from every walk of life. As I turned around to look behind me, I saw a tall, suntanned man wearing horn-rimmed glasses walking in my direction. Stopping directly in front of me, he looked down with a broad smile and asked, "Are you Miss Dickson?" "Yes," I answered, sighing with relief. Thus I met Aimee, Del Miller's head trainer.

Aimee turned out to be a very warm person, easy to talk to. He looked to be in his late fifties but could have been older, as he obviously took good care of himself. He was born in the French-Canadian area of Ontario and lived there until his early twenties; then he came down to America to work with the harness horses. As we drove along we chatted about my journey coming over, and when we neared the Meadowlands, Aimee informed me that I would be staying with the racetrack manager and his wife and daughter. John and Mary Peters and their daughter, Wendy, met me at the door and invited me into their spacious apartment, which was built over a block of garages with a grand view overlooking the racetrack. I was to be their guest for the next month.

I was now taking the big jump into harness racing, eagerly learning about pacers and trotters. To accommodate the horses at the track, the Meadowlands had a complex of twelve barns, each with twenty stalls. The barns were very different from the stables in England. My first impression was that they looked like airplane hangars, with the stalls grouped in the center and with a closed-in walkway around the perimeter for hand-walking the horses. I discovered that the walkway was very useful on cold winter mornings.

Standardbred trotters and pacers are basically an American contribution to racing. Although harness racing is extremely popular in France and Italy, it is still fairly new in

England. Of course, a horse is a horse, pretty much the same whether in England or America, and having driven ponies at home quite a bit, this part was not too difficult for me. I think the whole business depends on a good set of hands. I like to think my own are strong and capable, accustomed to controlling high-spirited horses on wild horseback rides over the fields, or being wrapped around a pitchfork full of hay, or used to gentle a frisky colt to rein and bridle. At the Meadowlands I was placed in charge of three young Standardbreds, doing everything for them-grooming, feeding, cleaning stalls, and exercising the horses. Just learning the elaborate rigging of the harness for trotters and pacers took some doing.

I thoroughly enjoyed driving the jog cart used for exercising, especially the sensation of speed as I gained confidence in controlling the sometimes high-spirited Standardbreds. Flying around the exercise track, I would imagine winning a race as the crowd in the stands cheered wildly.

The two-year-olds in my charge were in their early stage of training, and as the weather turned colder it came time for us to take them by horse van down to the racetrack in Pompano Beach, Florida, for the winter months. Thus, a month after my arrival, Aimee told my fellow grooms and me to pack all our horses' tack, blankets, brushes, leg bandages, and other paraphernalia in a large wooden trunk painted in Del Miller's colors of gold and brown.

I was to travel with Arthur, a fellow groom. He had been very helpful to me, showing me the ropes in general, particularly how to harness a horse correctly and adjust and fit the hobbles on a pacer's legs. A pacer needs these hobbles to keep him in his proper pacing gait. Trotters, on the other hand, do not need hobbles, as trotting is their natural gait. Harnessing a Standardbred is very important-it can literally be a matter of life and death for the driver. When sitting in his sulky behind his horse, the driver has to have complete confidence in the groom who has done the harnessing. The slightest error can cause a very serious accident.

You cannot imagine how much preparation is involved in shipping a van full of horses. This was especially true of our very valuable Standardbreds. Their legs were bandaged for protection, the halters were padded with sheepskin as a precaution in case they hit their heads, and their bodies were covered with a lined rug.

On the morning we were to start our long journey of over twelve hundred miles, everything was prepared. The horses walked up the ramp into the van, which held altogether eight horses. They seemed to sense that they were embarking on a great adventure. Their ears were pricked forward, and they were whinnying excitedly at each other. Everyone was loaded safely and two men lifted the ramp of the huge van and secured it.

Arthur and I were to follow in a pickup truck. Mr. and Mrs. Peters were there to see me off. I had the feeling that we would not see each other again because I didn't think I would be returning to the area. I was genuinely saddened by the thought of leaving them, as they had been so kind and generous to me. There were tears in my eyes as we all gave a last-minute hug, and as we were driving down the road past the racetrack I leaned out of the pickup window to wave a last good-bye.

I must admit that my sorrow at parting did not last too long, for soon a feeling of excitement swept over me in anticipation of the months ahead. I had heard so much about the Gold Coast of Florida! Heading south on Route 95 I felt like a modern-day pioneer.

We drove through the spectacular scenery of the Smoky Mountains, covered with oak, poplar, dogwood, and other trees stripped of leaves for their winter rest. The only green to be seen was scattered undergrowth of healthy-looking wild rhododendrons. Occasionally we spotted deer foraging among the dead leaves for food. The sole visible human habitation appeared to be an isolated log cabin here and there on the side of a mountain, visible through the majestic trees. The cabins had a look of poverty about them, but they seemed to be a natural part of the mountain life.

The highway ran through spectacular mountain passes which had been carved from the rock. Looking out at those mountains looming above the canyon walls on which our road was perched, I had a sensation of going back in time. The beauty of the Smoky Mountains was beyond my imagination, but I also sensed something a bit sinister in their awesome beauty-a feeling akin to fear, inspired by the thought that these mountains could be deadly to the unwary. It flashed through my mind that if you were not familiar with the mountains, you could be lost, perhaps forever, as most of the trees and underbrush looked the same. There was also the chance of getting bitten by a rattlesnake, a bone-chilling horrible thought to me.

I glanced over at Arthur as he drove. He was twenty years old, a tall lad with blond hair, twinkling blue eyes, and a round, jovial face. However, he was extremely rotund, and I had to suppress a giggle when I watched him walk-his weight caused his shoes to be worn down on the outside of his feet, giving him a truly comical bowlegged, rolling gait. He did not talk very much, and I did not try to force any conversation. But at one point I noticed he was having trouble keeping his eyes open, so I suggested we stop for a cup of tea at the next rest stop.

Our tea break seemed to revive Arthur, and we both felt refreshed and ready for the next hundred miles. We arrived at Southern Pines a few minutes earlier than the horses. Here the horses were to have an overnight rest. They were unloaded from the van by Arthur and the driver, and each horse was put in a stall ready and waiting for them. I helped remove their rugs and bandages and settle them down for the night. We found a motel not far from our charges and, after eating a hearty dinner, I fell into bed exhausted from so many hours of travel.

The next thing I knew, Arthur was knocking on my door telling me to get up, as it was time to get going. To my delight, Arthur and the van driver had already fed and bandaged the horses (no rugs this time, as it was now warm weather), and the van had already left on the final stage of its journey to Pompano.

After breakfast and filling up with petrol, we drove back onto Route 95, always exceeding the speed limit a little. But no matter how fast we drove, everyone else seemed to pass us, whether it was a car or a huge tractor trailer! Along the way I saw signs leading to cities or towns I would love to have visited-Charleston, South Carolina, was one. But this trip I was working for someone and not meandering on my own, so we stuck to the beaten path. The next four hundred miles seemed to go on forever. The highway was mostly straight and the land flat. The trees now were mainly pines with an occasional palm on which I could see coconuts growing near the top underneath hanging leaves. Canals had been bulldozed along the side of the road to drain the water off the adjacent land. To get relief from this monotonous landscape, I looked for alligators. If I was quick I would sometimes spot one sunning on the edge of the canal and looking very formidable before it slid silently into the water as we sped by.

Another way to pass the time was to read the huge billboards adorning the highway, singing the praises of motels, restaurants, animal farms, and assorted other family tourist attractions. This helped alleviate the tedium but certainly did not enhance the somewhat limited beauty of the Florida countryside.

Finally, two days and more than twelve hundred miles from our starting point, we came to Pompano Park-indeed a welcome sight. I was amazed to find how different everything was from the Meadowlands. Here there must have been at least twenty-five horse barns. The stalls were back-to-back, each with an attached covered shed so that, in effect, each horse had his own little porch where he could be cool and look out and see the surroundings. The paddocks were covered with deep sand and tufts of grass but were surrounded by all kinds of beautiful hibiscus growing in abundance.

When we arrived, the stalls were all ready with good clean straw and sweet-smelling hay in the hay nets. We were happy to find that, despite their long journey, all of our horses had traveled well. Before we put them in the stalls, we hand-walked them to stretch their legs.

Aimee, who had traveled down to Pompano several days earlier to get everything prepared, informed me that I would be staying with Mrs. Gillespie, a lady whose husband had passed away very recently and for whom Aimee thought I would be good company. This suited me just fine-no living expenses except to buy my own food. Financially this would be a great help as I started to get on my feet. Already, I had managed to save the magnificent sum of two hundred dollars. Now that I had a little money in my pocket, I was more confident that I could make my own way in this land.

Chapter 7

Pompano Beach

As Aimee drove me across the road to my new living quarters I nervously wondered whether I would be imposing on Mrs. Gillespie. I was worried that, just having lost her husband, she might not really want to be bothered having a stranger in her house.

Turning into the driveway, we drove up to a small white stucco house. The front door was painted bright green, and the house was surrounded by lush hibiscus bushes and masses of colorful impatiens. Boxer dogs were barking excitedly from the kennels I could see at the side of the house. Hearing them, Mrs. Gillespie came out to greet us.

She was a silver-haired lady dressed informally in a T-shirt and shorts. My first impression was how dreadfully thin she was. Her clothes hung on her small stature and her knee caps were protruding; even her shin bones looked razor sharp. I raised my eyes to look at her face, and even though it was drawn and pale, her green eyes sparkled as she met us holding both arms out to welcome us into her home. My concerns evaporated as she ushered me inside the house with every appearance of being genuinely happy to welcome me. Greatly relieved, I wished Aimee a thankful farewell and told him I would see him first thing the following morning.

My room was small with a single bed, a chest of drawers, and a built-in closet. The walls were painted a delicate pink, and elegant lace curtains draped the window. Mrs. Gillespie, the house, and particularly my cozy room, radiated such a feeling of warmth that I was certain I would be happy here.

My new home was a seven-minute walk from the track, and I enjoyed the exercise. Basically, my work would be the same as at the Meadowlands except that now I would have two horses that I was to take charge of myself. One was Onex, a two-year-old bay gelding trotter, and the other was Lady, a two-year-old chestnut filly pacer. Now I could learn to train both types of Standardbreds.

Driving Onex up on the training track the first morning was a little embarrassing, as everyone working at the track had heard about this new dark-haired English girl and were curious to see what I was like. I could feel the eyes of the other drivers on me, but each one had a welcoming smile and a cheery "good morning" for me.

The main exercise track was one mile around with a smaller half-mile inner track tucked inside its perimeter. Close by was Pompano Park, where the actual race meetings were held in the evening. I drove around the mile exercise track in the jog cart behind Onex with the early morning sea breeze blowing through my hair. It was a fantastically exhilarating experience. My back still bothered me horseback riding, so I was especially pleased at the thought that maybe harness racing was the thing for me. Onex, too, was feeling fresh, holding his beautiful head high, his long mane blowing in the breeze, and his strong muscular body moving so effortlessly. Everyone could see that he was extremely pleased with himself.

I fell into a pleasant, hardworking daily routine with my two horses. Each would be driven about three miles, hand-walked for thirty minutes to cool off, bathed, and then finished off by a brisk brushing and bandaging of the legs. Finally, my charges would be returned to their stalls to eat a well-deserved breakfast of grain and hay.

We started training very early in the cool of the morning, which gave me several free hours in the afternoon. Aimee, who turned out to be a special friend, and I made good use of the afternoons, enjoying the beaches and exploring local points of interest. My favorite drive was along the coastline from Pompano to Palm Beach. The road was lined with large elaborate homes surrounded by exquisitely manicured gardens abundant with flowering shrubs and trees. Each house trying to outdo the others with its architectural design.

Another month went by, and both of "my" horses were right on schedule with their training, indeed showing great promise. One Tuesday morning Aimee came up to me while I was grooming Onex and said in his deep, rich voice, "Mr. Miller has decided to enter Onex in his first race-a one-mile trotting race for two-year-olds-and you are to drive."

I could hardly believe my ears! I was ecstatic with joy; never in a hundred years did I think I would get the opportunity to drive in a real live race.

Mr. Miller was something of a mystery to me. He was apparently very popular, but at the same time he was essentially a private person. I never had the opportunity to get to know him. All he ever said to me was "Hello, how are things going?" All I really knew about him was that he came from a family of modest means but had worked hard as a young man grooming Standardbreds. He saved his money and bought a young bay colt, broke and trained him, and went on to win big races in record time. The colt's name was Adios and he made history at the track.

The evening had arrived for my debut at actually competing in the harness racing world. My heart was pounding with agitation and my legs felt shaky. My whole body was limp; in short, I was a basket case. Onex and I were entered in the second race. He was in tip-top form, and I knew that, unlike his driver, he was sure of himself and raring to go. Despite my nervous state I was able to take some solace from the thought that Onex was completely fit and that I had checked and rechecked his harness, which I had scrupulously maintained in spit and polish condition. I was also thrilled that I would actually be wearing the gold and brown racing colors of Del Miller's stable.

Before the race, Onex trotted his two three-mile warm-ups in great style. Between each three miles I rested him for three-quarters of an hour in his stall, covering him with a blanket to keep him warm and supple.

There were seven other horses and drivers entered-all, I am sure, eager to win. I was to be in number three position at the

(70)

Warming up Onex at Pompano Park on race day.

starting gate. Driving up onto the track from the stable area towards the stands, my agitation gave way to a different emotion-a combination of pride and excitement, and wishing my Dad could be there. Trying to contain my own feelings was quite enough, let alone driving Onex, who seemed to know that this was his debut. The starting gate was mounted on the back of a car, which drove slowly in front of the horses until they were all in position with their noses about six inches from the gate. We settled in our positions behind the gate, and the car pulled away. We were off!

I urged Onex forward and sat in my sulky, intent yet alert, with a firm but sensitive hold on the reins. For the first half mile we were all jostling for position, but then the speed began to increase as we neared the last quarter mile. Using every ounce of my strength, I encouraged Onex with my voice and hands. He responded magnificently as we trotted faster and faster over the home stretch. The blood was pounding in my veins, and, as if from a great distance, I could hear the other drivers urging on their horses and cracking their whips amid the roar of the crowd from the stands.

Now three of us were neck and neck. The wheels of our sulkies were almost touching as we careened down the track at breakneck speed. Then, like a flash, it was over. A photo finish. Onex and I were third. Third place, by most standards, was not a great victory. But for me, it was as if I had won the race of races and I was on top of the world. It was a dream come true! Being able to drive in a harness race at Pompano Beach is truly a memory I will always cherish.

As I climbed out of the sulky, patting and talking to my hero, my fellow drivers shouted their congratulations to me. This meant a great deal to me. I felt that I was now one of them, a member of the select fraternity.

In the days after my great experience I was finally feeling good about life. In large part this was due to the wonderfully kind people I had met since arriving in America. Not least was Mrs. Gillespie, who was a lovely women and became a very good friend. I think I was good for her also. When she came home after work in the evening, instead of coming into an empty house, she would find me cooking dinner. She, too, enjoyed a good cup of tea. But we shared much more in common than tea, as Mrs. Gillespie worked as a secretary at a dog kennel near Miami and her hobby was taking her boxers to shows, where she was very successful.

The weeks seemed to pass so quickly. It was now the first week in April, and once again it was time for the horses to be shipped to a new track. So everything was to be loaded into the big van to head northeast, this time to Lexington, Kentucky. Arthur volunteered to drive me again. Over the past few months we, too, had become good friends. He was still a shy lad, not exactly what I would call talkative, but our friendship had warmed him and we actually chatted together as we drove north. So this trip was less tedious, and time passed quite quickly.

Nearing Lexington, I felt a twinge of nostalgia as we passed a town named London.

The Lexington countryside was certainly different from Pompano. Spring had just arrived and the trees looked fresh with their delicate new leaves. Daffodils and crocuses were just sprouting up through the new green grass. I was particularly overwhelmed by the horse farms and their 19th-century large brick houses, each with barns and paddocks surrounded by literally miles of black painted fences. They seemed to snake their way across the gentle hills and valleys, and sinuously glide into the distance. Every fence and every tree had been meticulously positioned and planted to complement the landscape. England has beautiful horse farms, but I had never seen any that could compare with those in Lexington, near the home of the famous Kentucky Derby. This was landscaping in its ultimate expression: hundreds of acres molded both to their own and to their owner's will.

Many of the trainers and horses were new to me, but again everyone was so congenial and helpful. We were to be in Lexington only one month before having to move on once again. I really did enjoy working with my two horses and the excitement of the harness racing world. However, at the same time, I was tiring of this life of a nomad, constantly following the seasons by traveling from track to track. As I reflected on my future, I considered more and more how pleasant it would be to settle where I could put down some roots and even become part of a community.

I had read extensively of the rolling Virginia Piedmont hunt country, and the idea of living there preoccupied my thoughts. So, when the month at Lexington was over and it was time to pack up and ship the horses off on their next journey, I finally decided not to join them in following the racetrack circuit. A friend sold me a 1965 Mustang at a reasonable price, so I was all set once again to be on my way.

The decision to leave my friends and my horses was heart-wrenching. My good-byes were truly emotional, and tears blinded my eyes as I climbed into my Mustang. However, I stuck to my resolve and headed east to Virginia to find myself a job.

Chapter 8

The Dog of My Dreams

It was incredible driving over the fabulous Allegheny Mountains, passing through historic Winchester in the Shenandoah Valley, through Ashby Gap over the Blue Ridge Mountains and finally into beautiful Middleburg.

Approximately 600 people live in the tree-lined village of Middleburg. It was established in 1787 by Levin Powell, a Revolutionary War lieutenant colonel and Virginia statesman. He is said to have purchased the land now constituting the village of Middleburg for two and a half dollars from Joseph Chinn, a first cousin of George Washington. The countryside surrounding Middleburg has gently rolling hills and immaculate horse farms, and in the distance to the west are the Blue Ridge Mountains.

About a year earlier, when still in England, I had watched a visiting American named John Gordon Bennett play polo. I knew he lived in the Middleburg area but had no idea of his address. On a whim, I inquired at the local petrol station if they knew Mr. Bennett. Middleburg is small enough that they did, I was directed to his home two miles outside of the village.

Instead of ringing him first, I impulsively drove straightaway to his house. As I turned onto a dirt road, there to the right stood an old white stone house surrounded by mown green fields with white board paddock fencing. I drove in between the stone pillars and up the drive, stopping the car outside the front door. Nervously, I got out, climbed the steps, and rang the doorbell. After a short wait the door opened, and there stood Mr. Bennett with his white hair and bright blue eyes. I introduced myself and he immediately shook my hand and, smiling, invited me into his home. I explained that I had been in the country several months and, as I was in Middleburg, I thought I would look him up.

Mr. Bennett could not have been more gracious to a stranger who had so unceremoniously deposited herself on his doorstep. He introduced me to his wife, who was tall and slim, with her dark long hair pulled back in a ponytail. We sat chatting in their sitting room over a cup of tea-and a good cup of tea it was, too!-then Mr. Bennett asked if I would like to see his polo ponies. He took me out to his barn and proudly introduced me to his horses. He had about forty of them, which kept three men extremely busy full-time. As we were walking back to the house Mr. Bennett, out of the clear blue sky, asked me if I would like a job exercising his polo ponies.

I really was taken aback that I should be so lucky to have just arrived in town and be offered a job. Keeping a calm exterior, I said, "Mr. Bennett, I would like to accept the job."

The Colonial Inn, where I would be staying, is situated on the main street in the heart of town and was managed by Mrs.

Mabel Waddell Monroe, a dentist's wife. Mrs. Monroe was an elderly woman, definitely motherly, I thought, as I followed her up the creaky oak staircase to my room. A pleasant sensation came over me as I beheld a high four-poster walnut bed and a dressing table with a stool and, on the far side of the room, a large wardrobe next to a chest of drawers. On the floor there was an old, comfortably worn carpet, and two spacious windows overlooked the main street below. I immediately felt right at home and was eager to start my new job the next day.

Driving through the entrance to Rutledge, the Bennetts' farm, I tingled with excitement. Everything looked so cared for. The trees were coming into bud and clusters of yellow daffodils lined the road.

My job was to help look after the ponies and to ride the very quiet ones, training them for their fast and sometimes hazardous games of polo. I would be working with two experienced polo players named Hector and Pedro. Hector was a young, muscular, dark-haired man, who was married with two small children and lived in Middleburg. Pedro was older, also with two children. He had a chiseled face, lined and craggy from constant weathering by the sun. Even though he was a man in his late sixties, his body, always clothed with chaps from the waist down, looked strong and capable.

The three of us worked at one end of a large barn with Mr. Bennett's polo ponies. At the other end, Buddy, a cheery, red-haired, native-born Virginian, took care of Mrs. Bennett's pleasure horses. Mrs. Bennett was the picture of elegance when riding one of her mounts. She always wore polished black riding boots, fawn jodhpurs, a Harris tweed hacking jacket, and a cream shirt, all bought in England. The tack the horses wore was also made in Walsall and shipped over to the Bennetts.

Early in the morning before going to work, I would pop into the Coach Stop, a local restaurant, to have a cup of coffee and a piece of toast. It was there that I met Bob, sitting with other horse people at the counter having his breakfast. The first time I saw him he said, "Hello, nice morning." I politely answered, "Good morning."

The following week we just happened to be walking into the restaurant at the same time. We sat next to each other at the counter. For breakfast Bob had bacon, eggs, toast, and coffee and I had my usual toast and coffee. I had begun to drink coffee, as somehow the waitress could not make a good hot cup of tea.

Over breakfast we chatted about the weather and the area. Bob went on to say he had been born just a few miles away and horses had been his whole life. He competed in horse shows and bred mares and foals, and also owned several race horses which he entered at the racetracks in West Virginia and Maryland.

Even though Bob was not good-looking, he had something about him that was appealing. He was a lot older than I, but that did not bother me. His hair was a fine light brown combed back and slightly thinning on the top. His face was round and weathered with thick eyebrows and vibrant brown eyes.

Over the next year we went out together several times a week, and I found Bob was slowly creeping into my heart and I into his. He seemed to be a caring and a genuine person. As the months went by, we fell in love with each other. Ultimately, we decided we would drive down to Fort Lauderdale, Florida, and get married quietly. We married on December 12, 1967.

Meanwhile, I was beginning to meet other people in Middleburg. One acquaintance was Josephine, an English lady of obvious refinement, who had moved to Middleburg years earlier after her husband's death. I mentioned to her that I would love to adopt an Alsatian puppy, the English name for German shepherds. Her face lit up and she said, "Oh, Pam, I've just read an advertisement in the local paper, 'Six-week-old German shepherd puppies for sale.'" We spread the newspaper on the kitchen table and excitedly looked for the advertisement so that I could get the telephone number.

The German shepherd breed is a pure and ancient one. They are descended from the sheep dogs of Germany and have remained a pure type, possessing natural beauty. The breed might never have been known in England if it had not been for World War I. The Germans had used the breed for sheep dogs, but when the war broke out, they trained them as messengers and carriers of Red Cross supplies for the injured soldiers. Some of the dogs strayed and were found by the British soldiers, who brought them back home after the war. These dogs were the original founders in England of this breed.

At the outbreak of the Second World War in 1939, there was an appeal for trained dogs and experienced trainers. They were needed to work with the Air Force and Army. A number of German shepherds and trainers were enlisted. These early recruits were soon able to pass on their knowledge to others in the forces. They performed an incredible service for the country and saved a great number of lives when working with rescue parties, doing mine detection, and guarding aerodromes.

German shepherds are international. They are seen all over the world and top all other breeds with their exceptional protection and the companionship they give. No other breed possesses a keener sense of hearing or the uncanny sixth sense of knowing when danger is near. They are always on the alert and ready to give the alarm. Their protective instincts make them ideal as guard dogs and companions for children.

Although they are large, German shepherds are seldom clumsy. They are never as happy as when carrying out their master's commands. They thrive on working and are very unhappy if they are kept in a kennel. The German shepherd is basically a working dog, capable of great endurance and adaptable to any climate. Their beauty, intelligence, and aptitude for being trained have placed them among the more popular breeds.

In choosing a puppy, a safe guide is to inspect the parents to see if they are sound and healthy. A soft brown eye always gives a kinder and more pleasing expression. Color is secondary, as the colors change as the dog gets older. When picking a puppy up he should feel firm and solid, but the skin should be loose. The legs should be straight and strong with elbows fitting close to his body. The bones on his legs should be strong. The body should be deep and solid. The feet of young puppies, like the knees, are large and out of proportion. They should be round and the toes well arched. The nails should be short and black.

It is very important to examine the mouth. The teeth of the upper and lower jaw should meet, with the upper slightly overlapping, but touching the lower. If the upper jaw protrudes in front of the lower jaw it is termed "overshot," and if the lower jaw protrudes in front of the upper jaw it is "undershot." Both are extremely bad faults in a dog whose appearance matters.

I really wanted a black, silver, and tan dog, if not a sable with darker markings. I did not want a puppy with large or heavy ears, especially if they were wide-set and carried at the side of the head. I needed to choose a puppy that ran towards me with confidence and trust, rather than one that hung back and had to be coaxed to be friends. These were all the qualities I was looking for in a puppy.

A Mrs. Cramer answered the telephone when I called the number in the advertisement, and she gave me directions to her farm situated at the top of the mountain near Marshall, a small town nearby. One thing she forgot to mention was how appalling the lane would be leading up to her farm. Driving up the mountain, I encountered deep culverts winding back and forth across the dirt lane, unmistakable reminders of many rainstorms from previous seasons. Making my way precariously, I managed to maneuver my Mustang up the treacherous lane, hoping that when I arrived I would find that the puppies had the qualities I so much wanted. After a hair-raising few minutes, I eventually reached the farm, situated on a very choice piece of land overlooking the panoramic Fauquier County countryside.

Mrs. Cramer was waiting for me, surrounded by two huge, friendly German shepherds and eight of the most beautiful, fat, fluffy, and healthy-looking puppies I had ever seen. We introduced ourselves and sat on the grass to play with the puppies. They scrambled all over me, overwhelming me with kisses. I threw little sticks and leaves for them to chase and their little legs ran quickly, as each puppy tried to outrun the other. Sometimes their legs did not do what their brains would ask and they fell over each other, gamboling like wind-up toys. Then they would pick themselves up and scurry to rejoin the others, gently pulling at each other's ears and any other part of the body they could grab hold of with their tiny teeth. It was a sheer delight watching them play.

Both their parents were silver and tan, big and strong and beautiful. Even more important, I could tell that they had wonderful temperaments-exactly what I was looking for! Mrs. Cramer informed me that she did not show her dogs, but bred them for their temperament, looks, and soundness.

All the puppies were precious, and it was almost impossible to choose one. However, there was a certain something about one of the males. I do not know what it was, .but picking him up and holding him close, I said to Mrs. Cramer, "This is the one I would like to have. How much is he?" "I would like thirty-five dollars for him, please, Pam," she replied in her distinctive Virginia accent.

Elated at the price, I found myself the proud and excited owner of a beautiful black, silver, and tan puppy. Putting him in my car next to me on the front seat, I said good-bye to Mrs.

Rocky at six weeks.
As you can see, he was very tiny when I brought him home.

Cramer and made my way back down that incredible lane, heading directly to Dr. William S. Rokus's veterinarian clinic in Leesburg for my puppy to have his first of a series of three vaccinations. Dr. Rokus was originally going to be a neurosurgeon, but then his own sporting dog was injured and he healed it. This event, and his love for animals, dictated his destiny.

Rocky was to be my puppy's name. Back home my Dad and I had always watched boxing together on television, and our favorite boxer in those happy days was Rocky Marciano, the world heavyweight champion.

Spring was the perfect time to start my life with Rocky. I would be able to take him to work with me, as I was now working for Bob, helping take care of the horses. I seemed to be working harder and putting in more hours than I had anticipated, but I was determined I could find the special time needed with my new puppy.

The first night Rocky was home he cried a lot, missing his mom, brothers, and sisters. I put him in the kitchen with a blanket to lie on, a bowl of water, and the radio playing low, soothing music. After having such a busy day, he finally fell asleep.

Rocky awakened early the next morning when I opened the kitchen door. He ran to me with cries and a wagging tail. I scooped him up in my arms and held him close. I opened the back door to take him out and put him down gently on the grass, encouraging him to go to the bathroom. I followed this procedure at least six times a day-first thing in the morning, after his meals (I fed him small meals three times a day), after his nap, and the last thing at night before bed.

Training a puppy is very much like bringing up a child. You need patience and love, and I have plenty of both. With patience Rocky quickly learned to be housetrained, and after a few days he responded to his name. I tried to avoid correction by anticipating his needs. As young as he was, I took him everywhere, whether it was into the horse barn where I worked or just to the post office to collect my mail from England. Rocky was my constant companion. It is wonderful how much love puppies can give. With that look of adoration in their eyes, they can create in you a marvelous feeling of being wanted.

The way I handled Rocky at this stage would affect him for the rest of his life, so I needed to take things slow and easy, enabling him to enjoy his puppyhood but at the same time talking to him and showing him different sounds and objects.

Six weeks to me is the ideal age, for Rocky had not had time to form any bad habits and I would be able to mold his character just the way I wanted him. His parents, I had seen, had an intelligent strain. Simple training would become his everyday life, and he would automatically be obedient, as he was being brought up the right way.

There were times when he had to be left on his own. He cried and was a bit loud. It was very important that I tell him to be quiet. He soon learned to be content when he was left to lie in his bed.

I find it is never too early to start simple training. The difference between right and wrong can be indicated by tone of voice. Nothing more is necessary with a sensitive breed like a German shepherd, but it must be done instantly. Rocky, at this age, had a very short memory. I would watch him and try to catch him in the act of doing something wrong, then correct him. He associated the correction with this act. When Rocky made the same mistake twice, I corrected him in the same manner, and he remembered. I felt I was winning the first round.

I lavishly gave him praise and rewards in the early stages of his training. I kept the commands short and simple-sit, down, stay, and walk to the heel on the lead. Gradually I introduced right and left turns and finally about-turns with occasional sits.

Having perfected walking to heel on the lead, I detached the lead without Rocky's realizing it and then went through some of the movements with Rocky free. I did not do this until I felt Rocky was 101 percent ready. I wanted to keep him happy and maintain his trust.

It was an adventure for us both walking over the fields and down the bridle path, into the woods. Each turn was a new experience for us. We would come across chipmunks in the stone walls, chasing each other in play. When they saw us, they scampered back into their holes and, once in safety, would turn and peep out. Cottontails would hop and jump back into their burrows. Occasionally we came across a herd of deer, which raised their heads inquisitively, pricked their long ears forward, then turned and scampered over the field, bounding lightly over the paddock fence as they disappeared from sight.

The first time Rocky saw these creatures, his instinct was to give chase. I told him in a moderate tone of voice, "Rocky, no." Still looking at them, he hesitated as if he was going to give chase, so I repeated, "Rocky, no." He looked at me with innocent eyes as if to say, "Are you sure I can't chase them? It would be so much fun." Patting my leg to encourage him to follow, I said, "Rocky, come," which he did, with reluctance, but he followed my wishes.

When I spoke to him, it was softly or in a normal tone, as a dog's hearing is far more sensitive than that of a human. Shouting at a dog makes it become cowering and unresponsive.

The weeks were passing very quickly and, before I knew it, Rocky was twelve months old. His body was changing from the fluffy puppy into a gangly, long-legged young male with large ears too big for his head and body. His color was changing from a dirty cream on his front legs and chest to a lighter tan, and in the black on his back a few silver flecks began to appear. I was really pleased with the way he was developing; perhaps after all I really had the dog I had been dreaming of. His temperament with Bob and children who came to visit the house was perfect. He showed no signs of aggression and acted as if everyone had come to see him, and only him.

One evening, after a particularly busy day working with the horses, the situation I was in began milling around in my mind. For the last week Bob had been short a groom, so that meant I had to start work earlier in the morning and move a little faster to get through the day. When I met Bob, he gave the impression he was a successful businessman, but in only a few months of marriage I had seen he obviously was not. He had financial difficulties with his horse business.

I was beginning to feel that he married me for one thing-to work. He needed a person he did not have to pay. We were literally living from hand to mouth, as it turned out, and he possessed a violent temper and unpredictable personality. I could not conceive that I had made such a terrible mistake. I was beginning to feel a total failure, and I was struggling to survive. I had risked everything to come to the United States, and here I was married to a man I was growing to dislike.

On this particular evening, Rocky was lying on the carpet in the kitchen. He seemed to sense I was upset. As I turned my head, he got up and walked towards me. With tears in my eyes, I bent down and put my arms around his neck, nestling my face into his thick hair. Gently he turned his head and licked me on the cheek. That little lick made me feel so much better that I decided I had better stop feeling sorry for myself and be strong. I hesitated for a moment and said in a quiet voice, "Rocky, it is time for your first serious lesson."

I picked up my leather lead from off the coat hanger on the porch and beckoned Rocky to come with me. He jumped up excitedly, for he thought this was to be his regular run. We began in front of our two-story, 1920s stone house, which was surrounded by trees and shrubs. The area I chose, on the lawn in front of the house, was perfect, as it was flat and clear of trees.

Very quickly Rocky learned to sit and stay. I put him into position and said, "Rocky, stay." As soon as I moved away, he got up to follow me. Gently but firmly, I put him back in position and said, "Rocky, stay." This time he stayed. He was not sitting in the best position, but the main thing was he that was sitting and staying. I knew I could straighten him up a little later in his training. I used the same method with down-and-stay and stand-and-stay, varying the length of time he was to be in those positions, using my voice and hand signals.

The next step was the recall. With Rocky in either the sit, stand, or down position, I would tell him to stay. Then I would walk to the end of the lead facing him, wait a few seconds, and in an enthusiastic voice say, "Rocky, come," encouraging him as he came running towards me. I pulled in my lead so he came to a stop directly in front of me, and I told him to sit. Rocky looked up at me with a very eager expression on his face. I praised him, telling him what a good dog he was. Changing my lead from my right hand to my left behind my back, pulling Rocky at the same time, I told him to heel so he came to be sitting by my left side.

I noticed when Rocky was learning these steps of his training that he was very alert and eager to learn; the previous months we had spent together really had put his mind in a relaxed way and given him confidence. He certainly had a good attitude. You will find that an obedient dog is a contented dog.

After every lesson, to keep things interesting, we would climb over the stone walls, walk down steep embankments, and walk along fallen trees or any other obstacle that came across our path. I encouraged him as we went along with kind words and lots of pats.

To finish off we would go down to a large pond situated in the field next to the house. He loved to play, trying to catch one of the many large fish that zigzagged through the water.

Retrieving was an important part of Rocky's early training, especially in the water. Initially, I would throw a stick in the water and encourage him to bring it back to me. He swam directly to the stick, opened his mouth wide, and grabbed it, then began to swim in the opposite direction from me. I called for him to come, but he kept swimming and, upon reaching the bank, he glanced back at me with a naughty grin on his face, then with a gigantic leap took off over the field. I pretended I did not want the stick and sat on the ground looking for a five-leaf clover.

That was more than Rocky could stand. He came running to see what I was doing, depositing the stick in front of me. Gently, he poked his nose into the grass to investigate, while I picked up the stick and, patting him, slipped my hand into my jeans' pocket and pulled out a small piece of biscuit, his favorite treat. From that time on, he brought me the stick immediately. Hereafter I would throw a ball and larger objects into the water for him to retrieve, which he did without hesitation.

Rocky was now sleeping by the side of my bed on a cozy carpet. One particular morning when I was sound asleep, I felt something wet touching my cheek. I opened my eyes slowly, and standing before me was Rocky, looking at me with his nose a fraction away as if to say, "Come on, Mom, it's time to get up." I smiled as I stroked his face, as he lowered his head and rested it on the bed cover. I felt so fortunate to have Rocky as a friend who not only liked to receive love but also liked to give it in return.

Rocky in training for rescue work.

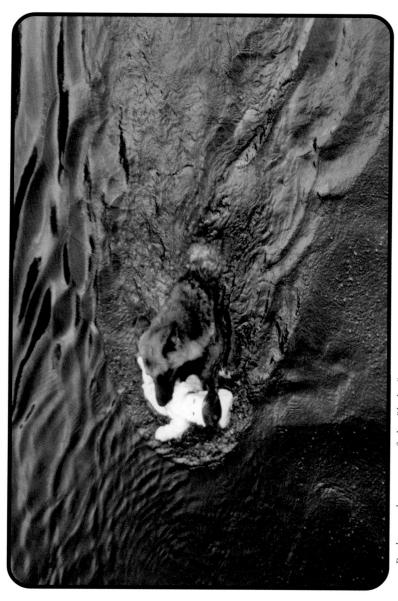

Rocky to the rescue of the "baby."

Mission accomplished!

Chapter 9

Rocky's Advanced Training

R ocky was now fifteen months old. Physically, he had developed by leaps and bounds. His body was becoming big and powerful, and his head had a noble look. I had conditioned him into perfect health, which meant he had the correct feeding, exercise, and grooming-none of which I had hurried.

His body was well covered with flesh, and he appeared muscular and supple. His long-reaching gait was smooth and graceful and was obviously capable of endurance, speed, and sudden and quick movements. The color of his coat had changed to a combination of black, silver, and tan, which varied slightly in shades according to the time of day. In the late evening when the sun was setting, the tan and black turned deeper and richer.

Having Rocky since he was a baby and being with him most of the time was really beginning to show remarkable results. My training technique was basically simple. I pointed things out to him and explained what I wanted him to do. The gentle repetition over the months had stimulated and strengthened his brain to understand the task at hand. The key combination was that he was anxious to please and had a remarkable ability to comprehend.

The first stages of his training lasted fifteen to twenty minutes per day, six days a week, taking every step slow and easy, making sure he understood each step before moving on to the next. The main thing was not to confuse his mind by pushing him too soon. That is where a lot of trainers make a big mistake. Being too anxious or impatient can put a dog back in his training for months, and sometimes they never get over it. My father said, "If you can't train a dog in six days a week, you can't in seven."

Sometimes I carried biscuits in my pocket to give him as a treat. He also received constant praise, even if sometimes he did not excel. I found it encouraged him to do better the next time. The main thing is, always be in a good mood when training your dog, as it projects straight into the dog's mind.

If one day you do not feel well, take the day off from training and go for a walk. It is amazing how much it will relax your body and mind; also your dog will have had a jolly good time. In fact, when Rocky was training so well, I would often skip a day or two and take him for walks over the fields or swimming in his favorite pond. It was my way of keeping him fresh so he would not get bored.

Rocky was the perfect age to advance with his training. A dream I'd had since a child was to own and train a dog like Lassie and Rin-Tin-Tin, the two original wonder dogs. I wanted Rocky to perform in front of children and adults. I tried to think of feats that children would enjoy and, at the same time, would educate them.

One day we had just run through Rocky's basics. Everything was effortless for him, and he looked very impressive in that special way people love to watch.

I put Rocky in the down position and stood in front of him. Bending over, I asked him to crawl. At the same time I was stepping backwards with my fingertips zigzagging through the short grass. His first reaction was to stand and walk towards me. I put him back in the down position. "Rocky, crawl," I said. My fingers were just in front of his nose as a guideline to help him stay in the down position. He began to follow and started to move his legs and tummy along the grass, wagging his tail as he crawled. I was really pleased, thinking the children would love it.

Next, standing before Rocky as he was in the sitting position, with his eyes focused on mine and eager to listen to my every word, I bent over and held out my right hand to him saying, "Rocky, give me your left paw." Lifting it, I held his paw in my hand for a few seconds.

The next time I outstretched my hand and said, "Rocky, give me your left paw." Without any hesitation he placed his left paw in my hand. I used the same procedure to teach him to give me his right paw.

Over the weeks, as a follow-up, he learned to lie on his left and right sides. Later, during performances, to make the children laugh he rolled over several times, which he really enjoyed. He seemed to have a favorite feat each week, as he learned new ones to add to his repertoire. Running through his routine, I varied our movements so he would not anticipate my commands.

I was trying fun things, such as having Rocky turn in a circle, and bending over for him to jump over my back. He learned this with a broom handle placed across two buckets turned upside down. I ran with him and, as we approached the handle, said "Rocky, over." I was a little stiff but Rocky went over naturally as if to say, "This is easy and fun, Mom."

The next time he jumped by himself, gliding over effortlessly. Pleased with himself, he came and sat directly in front of me, with his tongue hanging out a little, ready for the next phase.

He learned to obey commands with voice and hand signals until he knew exactly what was expected of him. He then graduated to hand signals. My command "over" was the signal for him to jump over the object in the direction I pointed and return right back to me, sitting squarely in front of me.

I put Rocky in the sit-and-stay position. He waited enthusiastically as I walked a few yards away from him. Turning, I held two hula hoops two feet six inches off the ground and six inches apart. In an energetic voice, I said, "Rocky, over." He sprang into action, taking a tremendous leap through the hoops, landing on the grass two yards away. I wanted to teach Rocky a little of everything to fill a thirty-minute program, hoping in the future he would be good enough to give exhibitions.

The tractor shed was full of interesting junk, including a tarpaulin sheet. I carried it onto the grass and pegged each corner into the ground. I knelt down in front of the tarpaulin, held it a few inches off the ground, and asked Rocky to lie down beside me. I put my hand on his head to lower it near the ground, then said, "Rocky, crawl." Lowering my head and body, I started to edge my way under, encouraging him to come along as I went. His earlier training came in handy. He knew what to do and started crawling quickly to the other end. You might know who crawled out first. Excitedly he turned around to lick my face as I scrambled to my feet.

I tried to make use of anything that was in the tractor shed. I noticed a long, narrow beam and two benches. I carried them onto the grass and laid the beam twelve inches off the ground. Rocky and I stood at the end of the beam. To build his confidence, I held him by the collar for support and helped him get his balance on the beam. The difficulty would be learning to put one foot in front of the other. Stepping on the beam and moving forward, he began to wobble. I held him steady, and slowly he reached the end. Over the next few weeks he became more sure-footed, and I gradually made the beam higher to make it more challenging for him. Eventually, it was four feet from the ground. On command he would nimbly jump upon the beam and walk along on his own, without difficulty.

People love to watch a dog jump, so I thought a variety of obstacles would blend right into Rocky's performance. The broad jump, which I made from wood in the tractor shed, was composed of four boards, each four feet long, placed at four, six, ten, and sixteen inches high. The first time Rocky jumped over, I put the planks just a few inches apart horizontally, so he would get the idea that he had to jump long. When he accomplished that, and after I gave him lots of praise, I reset the boards fifteen inches apart.

Pointing out to him that the boards had been broadened, I positioned Rocky in the sit-and-stay position eight feet in front of the jump. Standing at the side of the jump midway between the boards, I paused, looked at Rocky, and gave him the command "over." With a tremendous burst of power he headed straight for the jump. All four feet left the ground as he flew through the air, landing quite a distance on the other side. Then he turned and sat intently, facing me.

The high jump was a little harder for me to build. There were two side posts with slots to allow the pieces of wood to drop down in between, easily but securely. This jump I had to make stronger and heavier so there was no chance of its crashing to the ground should Rocky accidentally knock it. This jump also started low, then I gradually raised the height to three feet, which Rocky managed to span without any difficulty. I hung a car tire from an apple tree three feet off the ground which he barreled through, bullet-like, showing how flexible he was.

The tractor shed was built into the bank of a field. In the front, near the doors, a ladder leaned up against the wall, with the top rungs resting on the gutter. One day I stood there, pondering: could I teach Rocky to climb up the ladder, walk over the tiled roof, and jump off the back side onto the ground two feet below? My thoughts were that if ever I gave an exhibition at my home, this would be a fantastic addition to the program. The ladder was not very high, and the roof was quite slanted, so there would be no danger of either Rocky or myself slipping and getting hurt. Rocky's previous training on the beam would help him negotiate up the ladder with confidence, and I felt it would not be too difficult for him to accomplish, but at the same time it would be a very awesome experience for anyone who was watching.

As I said earlier, Rocky was always very keen to learn more, and at no time would I ask him to do anything that was not safe. I brought the bottom of the ladder out from the wall to slant it, put one of my feet on the third rung, and placed both hands on the ladder to test it to make sure it was stable. I asked Rocky to stand-and-stay at the bottom of the ladder while I climbed up onto the roof. Once up safely, I turned and dropped on my knees to look down and asked him to come up. Using my voice and hands to encourage him, I said, "Rocky, come." He looked up at me, and immediately put one foot on the ladder. "Steady," I said. If I had not spoken, he probably would have tried to come up too fast.

He started to make his way slowly up the ladder. I could see him using his brain, figuring out where to put each foot, making sure it was on the rung securely before moving his other foot onto the rung above it. I coaxed him up gently, reminding him to stay "steady." He listened to my every word as he climbed to the top, then carefully stepped off the ladder onto the roof, looking pleased with himself and wagging his tail.

I praised him quietly as we both walked slowly and carefully up over the roof of the building and jumped off the other side. It was only then that I got excited and made a big fuss over him. I felt so proud that he was my dog.

I am sure that most of you have seen the beautiful Lippizan horses from Vienna doing their elegant Spanish step. For teaching Rocky the Spanish step, I chose a flat area on the lawn that was closely mown. Rocky was in the standing position with me on his right side. I positioned my left hand on his collar at the top of his neck. Leaning forward I reached for his right foot with my right hand, lifted it, and placed it slightly in front and below his nose. "High step," I said to him, keeping his foot in place for a second, then letting it go gently back on the grass. I then lifted his left foot and held it a second in place, telling him to walk slowly. I used this procedure for a few yards, and with each step he took he began to extend his foot himself. I kept my hand in front of his nose as a guideline and grasped his collar to help him balance. After a few minutes' practice each day, he soon was able to do the Spanish step on his own. Rocky looked pretty impressive as we stepped together in perfect harmony.

To bring Rocky's performance to a dramatic close, I pretended he had been a bad boy and aimed a toy blank gun in his direction, then fired. The smoke poured from the end of the barrel as I directed him to lie down on his side. You aren't going to believe what happened next. Rocky dropped down on his left side with his head on the grass. His legs began to twitch, he moved his head back a little, accompanied with low melancholy groans as if he really had been injured. I was really amazed at what had happened before my very eyes. On his own, Rocky hammed it up to accomplish exactly what I had been planning in my mind.

I never commenced training if I did not have sufficient time to complete a lesson, as it was imperative I finish up with a note of praise. I was often tempted to show Rocky off to my friends, but refrained until I was 100 percent sure he was ready. At seventeen months, Rocky had accomplished more than I could have ever imagined. We had developed and perfected quite an array of canine feats.

I always kept my full attention while we were training, and never allowed Rocky's to stray. I was expecting absolute obedience before I could venture to give an exhibition, as we would find all kinds of excitement in the strange surroundings and be performing in front of an audience. I must be thorough to be able to put Rocky and myself to the ultimate test.

My secret dream had been to own a German shepherd: one with a rare, exceptional talent; a dog I could train to high levels; and with the strength, temperament, and looks that would attract attention at first sight. In Rocky I had found this very dog.

Rocky demonstrating that not all dogs are colorblind!

Chapter 10

The Dog Who Read Minds

My imagination went into high gear. Rocky had achieved everything I'd hoped. Lying on the floor of that good old tractor shed were twelve-foot-long pieces of wood, and there happened to be some sandpaper sitting on top of the pile. I hand-sawed five pieces into four-inch squares, sandpapered the corners until they were smooth, painted them yellow, and numbered them one to five. I wasn't sure if Rocky would be able to read the numbers, but we could try. I began by setting number one in front of him, then said, "Rocky, point to number one." I placed his right paw on it, and repeated the direction several times until he set his paw on the block himself, pulling it slightly towards him.

The next day I positioned the same block on the floor and asked Rocky to point to number one. He did, without hesitation. After a lot of praise I put the number-two block three inches away from number one. I said, "Rocky, point to number two," and laid his paw on the number-two block. We repeated this several times, and he quickly learned to pull the number-two block out on his own.

The following day I rearranged the two blocks. I followed this method for the next ten days, until he had perfected his recognition of each of the other numbers.

People say animals are colorblind-to me that has always been questionable. I decided to put Rocky to the test.

I painted another five blocks in red, white, black, blue, and yellow. I laid all five blocks in a row three inches apart. I beckoned Rocky to come and stand beside me twelve inches in front of the blocks. My eyes and mind rested on the red block. Before I could speak, Rocky quickly put his right paw on the red block. I thought it was accidental, but I praised him and put the block back in position. My eyes and thoughts rested on the black block. Again before I could speak, Rocky put his paw on the black block. I was astonished. This time it couldn't be an accident, as he had to move his body over to the right to enable him to touch the black block. It was unheard of, a dog reading a person's mind; at least that was what I was always led to believe. There seemed no end to Rocky's capabilities.

Two weeks later I cut, sandpapered, and painted five more blocks, this time with a letter on each spelling R-O-C-K-Y. I put the letters in the wrong order, to give Rocky another test, to make sure he really was reading my mind.

We both stood in front of the blocks, my eyes and mind resting on the letter "R." Rocky pulled the letter "R" forward. I proceeded to think of the letter "O." Automatically Rocky's paw reached out and pulled in the letter "O." Not daring to stop in case we both lost concentration, I proceeded, and Rocky pulled out all five letters in the right order.

I could not control myself. I went absolutely out of my mind with excitement while hugging and praising Rocky, who appeared just a little bewildered at my obvious joy.

Over the last two years Rocky and I had learned so much together. It is very rare to find a dog like Rocky. Not only did he have a tremendous ability to learn and was able to accomplish extraordinary feats (even beyond the capability of film dogs who normally have a stand-in, as they are not capable of performing all the stunts themselves), but also he was a nice dog.

The time was February 1970, and Rocky was two years and one month old. I was so proud with our progress that I wanted others, particularly large groups of children, to see what my Rocky could do. He always seemed to enjoy performing for friends' children. But putting him before bigger audiences required some exposure in the way of publicity. So, on the off-chance that they might be interested, I rang the *Loudoun Times-Mirror* in Leesburg and told them about Rocky. They seemed very interested and said they would come and meet Rocky the very next day. Putting the receiver down, I could hardly contain myself. Of course, Rocky had been listening to my conversation as he lay relaxed on the settee.

As the next day dawned, the weather turned nasty, so most of Rocky's performance would have to be either in the barn or in the house. The reporter sent to visit us was Brett Phillips, and the article he wrote was published on the front page of the weekly newspaper, together with a photograph of Rocky. His article is reprinted here, with the kind permission of the *Loudoun Times-Mirror*.

FROM SCHOOLWORK TO BOGART
A DOG OF MANY TALENTS

If you were to come downstairs one morning with a bad hangover, and there was this dog standing around the kitchen counting things or selecting colors, or playing the role of Humphrey Bogart in his worst gangster movie, you would probably turn around and go back to bed for further recuperation. Even if you were in Pam Dickson's house in Middleburg. But if you were in Pam's home, that dog would probably still be there when you took your second fling at sobriety. Only this time he might be motoring backwards around the kitchen or practicing leapfrog, or doing some other unlikely thing. In this case, the dog would be Rocky, a remarkable canine who, at the age of two, weighs in at 110 lbs., and who acts like he should be a first-year kindergarten student instead of a purebred German shepherd.

Rocky's abilities are the result of patient training administered over the last two years, during which the husky, black, silver, and tan shepherd has emerged from being another playful pet into a resourceful performer.

Pam came to be interested in dogs honestly, having operated a kennel in her native

England before coming to the United States. Spurred into action by his mistress, Rocky went into a series of maneuvers which included heeling, charging bullet-like through a hoop held three feet off the ground, laying first on one side and then the other (he knows his left from his right), leaping without a command over his mistress's back, when she leaned over. This particular act could prove distracting for someone trying to scrub floors, but its entertainment qualities are obvious.

Following his more physical perfor-mance, Rocky retired to the kitchen for some schoolwork. Pam laid out five different color blocks on the floor and instructed Rocky to select the red one. He did without hesitation. She repeated color commands several times, including once when she placed a light yellow block and a white one side by side-the dog picked out the yellow one immediately. That done, Pam had us write down a color on a piece of paper and give it to her. She studied the piece of paper and, without her having said a word, Rocky went to the blocks, surveyed them, and picked out the color block named on the piece of paper.

Pam then switched to numerals, lining up white blocks numbered from one to five.

Rocky was asked to pick out the number three, which he did-then selecting several others as requested. Pam then turned the blocks over to hide the numbers, and the dog still picked the proper one. Asked how she managed to teach Rocky this variety in a year, Pam observed that "the only way to do it is with kindness and patience-lots of patience."

Actually, she said, some of the tricks were developed as an indirect result of things the dog had already learned to do. Such was the case with the colors-she first taught him to differentiate between numbers and then decided to see if he could apply the same concentration to colors. As it turned out, he could-and the experiment resulted in still another discovery. That was the most intriguing of them all-that Rocky is apparently able to sense what colors Pam is going to ask him to select, and will pick the right one out before she actually relays the order.

"I really discovered that only by mistake," she explained. "After I taught him to pick out colors, I started noticing that he would go to one before I told him to and he was picking out the ones I was thinking about. To be perfectly honest with you, I was amazed that he learned the colors and the numbers."

(112)

Rocky is obviously using both the sight and sound senses, and apparently has no preferences between them.

Pam says she is quite interested in having Rocky perform for children, underprivileged or otherwise, in the county. "Rocky loves children and seems to enjoy performing for them more than anyone else," she said.

The scenario Rocky likes more than any is the one in which Pam picks up a cap pistol, admonishes him jokingly for being a "bad dog," then plugs him: Rocky rolls his eyes, staggers around a bit, issues a long groan, and then flops down "dead" looking like he might at any second crack, "You got me, you dirty rat," a la Bogart. His act finished, Rocky wandered off to play with a badly mangled football while Pam explained that the rainy day had made him a bit sluggish.

No apologies were necessary-Rocky is something else.

Chapter 11

Rocky's Debut

After publication of such a splendid article, you can imagine the overwhelming response Rocky and I received. Letters came from people all over the county wanting to meet Rocky and asking that he give a performance at their schools and nursing homes.

One of these invitations which I accepted stands out vividly in my mind. It was from the government of the District of Columbia Social Services Administration. They wanted Rocky to perform at Junior Village, a home for orphan children and older people who needed constant supervision. I told Eula Delaine, the administrator, that Rocky and I would love to visit the home. We decided Friday at half past one would be good for us both. Mrs. Delaine was especially pleased when she learned there would be no charge for the performance.

The exhibition was to be held in a big hall with a stage large enough to give Rocky plenty of room to extend himself while performing. The hall was filled with children from age four up, and there were a number of elderly people in their seventies and eighties. I was being given chance to prove the overpowering effect a dog can have on a lonely or sick person.

Rocky evokes smiles and tender emotions
from these gentle grandparents.

Rocky and I climbed up the steps onto the stage. Smiling, I glanced around at the audience and saw that all eyes were resting on Rocky. He had such stage presence. Even though he was just sitting, I could see he had captured their hearts.

I began by telling them about Rocky-where he was born, his age, and a little about how he was trained. We began to run through our routine, beginning with his left and right paws, lying on his left and right sides, and crawling along on his tummy. They were interested to learn how I taught Rocky to sit, stay, down, stand, and come when called.

I chose Pat and Larry, both about eight years old, to hold the hula hoops. Rocky jumped through them effortlessly, and when he landed, shrieks of approval rang through the hall.

I positioned the children next to each other, and asked them to bend over, low enough for Rocky to jump over them. He was ready and waiting. I beckoned to him, and he sprang into action, taking off at the right time and gliding through the air over their backs. Upon landing, he turned quickly and ran to the children, who were still bent over, and pushed his nose in between their little hands to lick their faces as if to say what fun he was having. I can still hear the giggles and laughter from those children.

I thanked Pat and Larry for doing such a fine job helping me, and they went down to sit by their friends, who were excitedly nudging and whispering to them.

The biggest test of all was whether Rocky and I could manage to do the colored blocks routine correctly. This was our first time in front of a large audience. Taking a deep breath I noticed a young man about sixteen, standing by himself at the back of the hall. When I beckoned to him, his face turned bright red. Then, as if by magic, his companions started to cheer and clap, encouraging him to get up on the stage. Very self-consciously, he began to walk toward me. I held out my hand and took his in a handshake. His name was Paul.

Paul placed the colored blocks in a row. I explained what we were going to do, and added that I must have absolute silence. "Paul, what color would you like Rocky to choose?" I asked. "Red," he answered.

It seemed as if Rocky didn't even have to think. His paw automatically pulled out the red block. The children watched in disbelief, their eyes beginning to bulge.

"Paul, choose another color," I said. "Blue," Paul answered confidently. Again without any hesitation Rocky pulled the correct block forward. The children began to sit on the edge of their chairs to get a little closer. They didn't want to miss a single thing.

Rocky went through all the colors and numbers without wavering a single moment. My biggest demand on Rocky was to spell his name. I asked Paul to mix the letters. I asked the audience to keep still and very quiet, as we needed complete silence to enable Rocky to spell his name. My mouth had gone a little dry with excitement, and my tummy wasn't feeling very good either. Taking another deep breath, and bending over, I said to Rocky, "Come on, lad, you can do it." It seemed he knew exactly what I was saying, and he licked my cheek.

Standing by Rocky's side, I directed my eyes to the letter "R." He pulled it out. My eyes moved to "O." He pulled that out. Then on to "C" so quickly and then the letter "K." That left the letter "Y." Rapidly he rested his paw on it, pulling it forward. The audience cheered and clapped wildly, and Rocky joined in barking on command. He knew how clever he had been.

Once everyone had quieted down, Paul left the stage and went to sit among the other boys and girls.

At the end of the program, I said I was going to pretend Rocky had been a bad boy. I aimed the toy cap gun about five yards away from him and fired.

Rocky began to stagger, stumbled a few yards, and then fell over on his side, twitching his legs and whining loudly. In all the months we had practiced this particular feat, he had never put on such an act. He was absolutely incredible! Apparently the more people who saw him, the better he performed.

After the show, I took Rocky offstage to meet his new admirers. Everyone wanted to touch him.

There was one little boy in particular, whose name was James. He looked to be about six years old, his hair was black and curly, and he was what I call a beautiful child. His nose was little and cute, and his eyes were a deep brown. His ears looked "alert," while his body was small and fragile. He had caught my eye during the performance sitting in the front row where his friends were explaining to him what Rocky and I were doing. I realized he was blind.

After the performance, James timidly asked if he could feel Rocky's face. I was overwhelmed by my emotions, and tears welled up in my eyes. Bending down by Rocky's side, I gently took the little boy's hand, placing it on Rocky's face. With his little fingers, he gently touched the dog's wet nose, then carefully worked his hand up around Rocky's smooth cheeks and to the dog's eyes and forehead, and gradually his fingers caressed Rocky's soft, silky ears. Suddenly, James put his arms around Rocky's neck and nestled his face into the dog's thick coat, saying softly, but with tremendous feeling, "I love you, Rocky."

After a few seconds he said to me, "Pam, can I feel your face?" With tears still in my eyes, I took his hand and placed it on my cheek. He began feeling my face and hair, his little fingers touching every inch carefully, ending up softly holding the end of my nose. A lovely smile came over his face as he flung his arms around my neck, hugging me with all his strength. My own arms encircled his fragile body as my heart went out to him.

I can't truly recall ever being overwhelmed with more compassion than at that moment as we held each other. He was a little blind child without a real home and family, yet with a tremendous ability to overcome his disabilities.

Driving back home to Middleburg with Rocky lying contented on the back seat, I was filled with the thoughts of all the hours Rocky and I had spent together, and in the last hour I had been rewarded more than I could have ever imagined. Not only had the children enjoyed Rocky, but the older people had too. As for James, I will never forget his smile and the sensation of his arms around me. I felt that Rocky and I had put a little happiness into these people's lives.

Chapter 12

Hurricane Agnes

It was July 2, 1972, when Hurricane Agnes passed through Loudoun and Fauquier counties, leaving behind fallen trees, swollen creeks, and many severely damaged or destroyed homes.

Aldie, established around 1780, is a small village in Loudoun County, approximately forty miles west of Washington, D.C., on Route 50. A normally serene creek called Little River runs by Aldie, winding its way east and ending up in the Potomac River. The overnight torrential rains and winds of Agnes had swollen the Little River into a rampage-overflowing its banks several feet above normal, flooding fields beyond recognition, and sweeping trees and bridges along in its fast-moving current.

On the east side of Aldie, situated a few yards away from the river, is an old wooden house named the Gate House. Emma Costello, a lady of modest means and a long-time respected resident of Aldie, lived there alone. Her nine children had grown up and moved away.

I had never met Mrs. Costello, but learned of her catastrophe from Mr. Franklin Payne, the Aldie postmaster. He said she had lost all her belongings in the flood. A deluge of water had engulfed the house, rising to the second floor, leaving behind deep mud on the floors, furniture, and curtains. Several of the congregation from Aldie Methodist Church were helping to repair, wash, and clean the house.

Today was July 5, and I thought if my husband Bob, Mary and Angela (my friends from England who now lived in the D.C. area), and I planned together, we could organize a benefit to aid Mrs. Costello. The idea went over well with them, and it was decided we would invite everyone we knew by word of mouth. The only entertainment was to be a demonstration by Rocky.

Mrs. Worthy Caulk, a neighbor and friend who wrote for the *Washington Star*, said she would write an article about Rocky and mention the benefit to be held July 9 at half past one in the afternoon.

Previous to our big day I spent time preparing the area in which Rocky was going to perform. I wanted to organize all the equipment for the event and put it into position where the audience would be able to see Rocky clearly. Bob trimmed the hedges and cut the grass so that when our guests drove in through the gate entrance, everything would look beautiful.

Sunday was going to be one of the most special days of my life-a day in which Rocky and I would be performing in front of our friends and neighbors and, I hoped, would earn a little money for Mrs. Costello.

That morning proved to be clear and quite cool for the month of July. I suggested to Bob that I have the morning off from working in the barn, so Rocky and I could relax and prepare ourselves mentally. Bob, I am afraid, did not agree with me. He said I was needed at the barn. Instead of being strong and refusing to go to work, I obeyed, to save any trouble.

The morning dragged on and things were going very slowly. The exercise girl who rode the horses was late, putting me further behind. That meant I arrived home later than the expected time. As I turned into the drive back at the house, I could see people had already begun to arrive. I began to panic, rushing into the house, and there standing in the kitchen were Bob, Mary, and Angela. Simultaneously they asked, "Where have you been?" That was all I needed to hear! I was tired, fed up, and overanxious about the performance. I started to cry. I couldn't help myself, and burst out, "If I hadn't have had to go to work, I wouldn't have been late!" I glanced out of the window through tearful eyes to see more cars arriving.

Looking at the clock, I could see I had only five minutes. I knew I didn't have time to shower. Running upstairs into the bathroom with Rocky at my heels, I quickly changed clothes and splashed cold water on my face to cover up my red eyes. I couldn't believe this was happening, today of all days. I breathed deeply a few times to get my composure. I couldn't let Bob cloud my vision. Rocky and I had trained too long, and I had often dreamed of a day like today.

I had to think of Rocky, Mrs. Costello, and the people who had taken their time to come to our benefit. Unfortunately

(123)

Mrs. Costello herself could not attend because of her health. Walking downstairs into the kitchen, I glanced at Bob, who said, "Hurry up, everyone is waiting for you." Poor Angela and Mary; I could tell from their expressions that they felt so bad for me. Smiling faintly, they wished me the best of luck.

Normally, before Rocky and I put on a show, it was I who was the leader, so to speak. Now, as we left the kitchen to go outside to present Rocky to our guests, I was depending on his strength to carry us through the next thirty minutes.

Rocky's performance was perhaps his finest ever. He jumped, crawled under the tarpalin, walked along the narrow beam, rolled over, high-stepped, climbed up the ladder onto the roof and jumped off the other side, and ended up with his now famous death scene, with a miraculous recovery to enjoy his applause. After the performance Rocky circulated among the entire audience, carrying a bucket in his mouth. Who could refuse this request for donations from the star of the show himself? The upset before the show seemed long gone, as young and old people enjoyed meeting Rocky and watching him perform. Everyone gave generously. It was decided that Rocky and I would take the money in the bucket and give it to Mrs. Costello exactly as it had been donated.

Rocky and I pulled up outside Mrs. Costello's house. The rampaging river had now receded to its normal level, but it had left a trail of driftwood and rubbish on its banks.

I knocked softly on the front door, with Rocky standing by my side. The sound of footsteps on the bare wood floor grew louder as they came nearer. The old weather-beaten door opened slowly, and a small, older lady wearing glasses stood before us. She didn't know we were going to visit her, so it was a complete surprise to her when she opened the door and saw Rocky standing before her holding a bucket filled with money. Mrs. Costello became overwhelmed with emotion as she accepted the bucket from Rocky's mouth. She sat down and patted Rocky and told him how kind he was, and how fortunate she felt in having such wonderful friends.

Looking up at me through her teary eyes, Mrs. Costello said, "Pam, I've always had a soft spot in my heart for German shepherds."

Rocky talking over business regarding his advertising for the bank with Mr. William Curtis, president of The Middleburg Bank.

Chapter 13

Houston

Rocky and I began to get much more deeply involved in entertaining than I had anticipated. I decided to make a short film of some of Rocky's special feats, the ones he could not do indoors. Perhaps this would have a special appeal to dog clubs and schoolchildren.

I had met a young man in Middleburg, David Rypka, who had a small movie camera capable of filming my project. I was to buy the film, write the script, direct, narrate, and choose the old records for the background music, while David would be the camera man and editor.

The movie featured Rocky in a lively display of tricks, demonstrating his now famous Spanish walk, followed by tracking a lost person, and scenes of how to rescue a child in distress.

In one sequence of the film, Rocky, with the aid of David Simpson, a real-life Middleburg policeman, tracks down a "wanted man." As the man runs from the house and climbs a ladder onto a roof from which he can escape, Rocky follows on his heels, agilely manipulating the rungs on the upright ladder.

The thief is finally caught after a harrowing chase across a field by the lawman and his dog. Children found this part terribly funny, but the film made their parents aware of the helpfulness of a trained dog in tracking lost children or rescuing them from a pond.

One evening I was watching television with Bob when an advertisement came across the screen, featuring a dog selling a product. "Why, Rocky could do as well!" I said, turning to Bob. "I think I will write to the advertising agent." The next day I put a résumé and photos of Rocky together and sent it off to the New York agency representing a major dog food. A week later I received a letter from the agency. I was very apprehensive in opening it. My fingers trembled as I ripped it open. To my delight, they were very interested in having Rocky represent them at a supermarket convention in Houston, Texas, in April. The letter ended with a request to call collect.

Our excitement grew over the next few weeks. Finally the day arrived to leave for Houston. I had invited my long-time friend Mary to drive along with Rocky and me. It would take us just over two days, covering twelve hundred miles, passing over the Appalachian Mountains, down to Atlanta, Georgia, then heading west to Shreveport, Louisiana, and finally turning south to Houston.

We followed the signs pointing to the Astrodome, which was situated across the road from the hotel in which we were to spend the next three days. Adjoining the hotel was a large field-perfect for Rocky. Forty thousand buyers were expected to attend the supermarket convention, and it was

Rocky's job to attract attention to our corporation's booth, where I would spend three afternoons.

There were hundreds of booths and thousands of men and women walking down the aisles, smartly dressed, carrying their briefcases, visiting the booths in which they had a special interest.

Our booth was mainly collars, leads, chains, brushes, combs, and doggie treats. People said Rocky was the main attraction at the convention, even though he spent much of his time in the sit-and-stay position. He was like a magnet; buyers who had come from all over the country were drawn to him, and they told each other about Rocky. Every sixty minutes he put on a little show.

One man opened a package of treats and gave one to Rocky. Immediately he spit it out, and everyone started to laugh. I couldn't believe what had happened. Keeping a straight face, I said matter-of-factly, "Rocky spit the treat out of his mouth because he is not supposed to accept food from strangers." Keeping my fingers crossed, I offered Rocky the same treat. He took it willingly, to my great relief.

While I was in Houston I had heard about the Shriners' Hospital for children. I phoned Jack Smythe, the superintendent, explaining that Rocky and I were at the convention and we would love to come and visit the children. We were invited to go the next morning. The nurses were anxiously waiting to meet Rocky. Nurse Joyce Kelly was the one chosen to show us around and introduce us to the children. I sat on the edge of the beds chatting with each child, while Rocky placed his paw on the cover to allow the child to stroke him. If their eyes had been full of sadness, when they saw Rocky they came to life, and a smile came over their face. Rocky had the power to get a response, even though the children were terribly ill.

A mile from the Shriners' Hospital was a school for emotionally disturbed and underprivileged teenagers. The nurse made arrangements for Rocky and me to visit the school. I was going to try to make this a very special program because a lot of these youngsters, I could see, had not been very fortunate in their lives. If Rocky and I could give them a little happiness, I would be glad.

People who live in other countries think America is paved with gold, but I'm afraid that is not always the case. Rocky and I had been traveling to different schools-several in large cities in the ghetto, others in small villages-and the poverty of many of those children was overwhelming. Some of them had never seen a dog, let alone touched one. The teenagers sitting before me looked helpless and lost, very much like those in the ghetto. The program was held in a classroom and about twenty young people were sitting slouched on their chairs. Barbara Ellison, their teacher, introduced me to them.

I glanced around smiling at everyone. Their reaction to me was as if I were nonexistent. I could read what was on their minds. They thought it was going to be just another boring hour. They were wrong. I was going to make it a program they would not forget, and an experience I hoped would fill their minds with nice thoughts.

(130)

Rocky-one magnificent looking dog.

(131)

I started my program by saying, "Good afternoon, ladies and gentlemen." A young lady stood up and said, "Thank you for calling us that." I felt the ice had been broken. I thought they would like to know a little about me, so I went back in time to when I lived in England, telling them about my horses, dogs, and the farm. I then told them about my arrival in the United States with only fifty pounds, and of course, when I bought Rocky. Some of the photos I had taken of Rocky were wonderful to prepare the teens for the film. The expression on their faces began to change from a "don't care" attitude to "tell me more."

The lights were dimmed as I started the film. Everyone had their eyes fixed on the movie. During each segment they sounded their approval, especially when Rocky climbed the ladder onto the roof and caught the criminal.

The climax of the film was a make-believe "Rocky party" at our house. Rocky and a little girl somehow managed to elude the group and go adventuring together. They wandered off in the direction of the river, and when they reached the bank-site of the earlier training session where Rocky had entered the water-the little girl decided to go wading. Rocky wanted no part of this. He stubbornly refused the child, who was urging him to go wading too.

She went anyway, carefully picking her way across to a likely-looking outcropping of rocks. Rocky watched, moving around nervously, keeping an eye on the child. Suddenly she slipped into a deep spot, and frantically clawed her way up to the rocky outcropping, pulling herself to temporary safety. Now she was wet and cold and uncertain how to get back.

Rocky watched, whimpering. The child put out a tentative foot, but couldn't touch the bottom. Because she was a self-reliant little girl, she was not very frightened-at least not as long as Rocky was right there in plain sight. But she began to be very cold and she began to cry.

Rocky recognized it as an appeal for help. He looked at her, then at the water (the river was running very fast from his angle), and, with obvious concern, entered the water. He swam across to the child, and she grabbed him around the neck. Together they splashed back to the bank and safety. The child wrung the water out of her dripping dress and rescued her shoes. Rocky, with a mighty shudder, shook himself more or less dry. The child, with her hand resting on Rocky's head, set off to rejoin the group-which by now had missed them and started looking for them.

They were greeted with cries of joy and some alarm (seeing how wet they both were). The child looked up at the adults and announced excitedly, "Rocky saved my life!" Rocky was engulfed in a stream of questions, pats, and applause. From the expression on his face you half-expected him to say, "It was nothing, really."

To my amazement, at the end of the film there was a standing ovation, and several of the teenagers shook my hand. I swelled up with pride, knowing my 120-pound German shepherd had melted the hearts of these young people.

I had left Rocky in a room next door until the end of the film I had made about him. With great pride, I asked if the young people would like to meet Rocky. Excitement broke out among them. They did not realize Rocky was in the school. Upon entering the room, Rocky looked very self-assured. The way his mouth was open a little, with his tongue slightly hanging out, gave the impression he was saying, "Here I am, wasn't I great?"

Each student had a question to ask, from what kind of food he ate to how long it took to train him.

In every show there always seemed to be one person who caught my eye. This time it was a boy about sixteen years old, who was standing in the background. I knew he was longing to come over to Rocky. Finally, he got up the courage and came forward. He bent down beside Rocky and gently stroked him, saying how big and beautiful he was, and how he had enjoyed the program.

Everyone thanked me and patted Rocky as they passed him to go on to another class. As I was packing up the projector, Mrs. Ellison said how much she had appreciated that Rocky and I had taken the time to come to her school. She added that this was the first time she had ever seen the young man, whose name was Paul, take an interest in a program. It had taken Rocky-a dog-to accomplish that.

Chapter 14

The Children's Party

Twenty miles north of Middleburg is Leesburg, and on the far side of town is The Paxton Memorial Home for Children. I thought it would be fun to invite the children from Paxton and the first-graders of Middleburg Elementary School over for a "Rocky party" one Sunday at half past one. I talked it over with Mary and Angela, and they agreed that it would be a lovely afternoon for the children.

When I was in town I happened to run into Mrs. Phelps, the headmistress of the Middleburg School, and told her of my plans for a Rocky party. She thought it was a wonderful idea, and she knew the children would like to come. It was decided the parents would bring the children in their own cars.

Then I phoned Paxton Memorial and talked to Mr. Buchanan, the director, about our plans for Rocky's party. He also was delighted with the idea, so it was arranged. The children would ride in the school bus along with their dormitory mothers.

The weather was perfectly beautiful as the school bus and cars drove into our drive. When they pulled up, the doors opened, and out tumbled little boys and girls ranging from four to ten years old. It was wonderful to see the anticipation on their faces.

We gave them a warm welcome and, taking the tiny hands of the youngest children, walked with them to seat them on the grass to watch Rocky's show.

Today was going to be a shorter program because we had games and a picnic to follow. Rocky and I played "Simon Says"-everything I did, Rocky did. We jumped over low jumps, turned in a circle, rolled over and over, high-stepped, climbed up the ladder, and finally concluded with his famous death scene, which Rocky did on his own.

The children's faces shone with glee as they watched the show. Afterwards they pushed and shoved to touch Rocky, while he put back his ears enjoying every pat.

Angela and Mary had organized games, so the children could take advantage of spending the sunny afternoon in the country. The sack race was my favorite, as they jumped and hip-hopped over the finish line-falling to the ground in a fit of giggles; others were playing ball or jumping over the jumps pretending to be Rocky.

I stood for a second to watch their faces, and saw that everyone was having a good time. We had planned ice cream, homemade cakes, chips, and punch, which covered a table under the shady oak tree. Angela rang a bell to let the children know the picnic was ready. The children formed two lines, tussling and pushing, until finally each child had a paper plate full of goodies and a shady place on the grass. All too soon the

Everyone had a jolly good time at Rocky's party.

A typical letter from one of Rocky's young fans.

afternoon came to an end. Feeling sad to see them go, we helped the excited and very refreshed boys and girls onto the bus and into the cars. We waved goodbye to them as they started down the driveway.

Rocky began to receive many fan letters from the children, addressed simply "Rocky, Middleburg, Virginia." I was really pleased with the results of the party, since Rocky and the children had obviously enjoyed themselves very much.

I had not been over to England for a year, so the following day I made plans. Before I knew it, I had boarded the plane at Dulles Airport and was heading across the ocean to my home country and beloved family.

During my holiday I saw an advertisement in the local paper: "For sale, six-week-old Jack Russell puppies." This was the same kind of small working terrier I had owned when I was a child. They were bred and named after the well-known Reverend Jack Russell, who was born in Dartmouth, England, in 1795. Russell became famous for his pack of small foxhounds which he hunted over the west country. Apart from his fox hunting, he was a good parish priest and, with his friendly manner and good temperament, was very popular with people from all walks of life.

In 1971 there were very few Jack Russells in America, and I thought Rocky would like to have one as a little friend. On impulse, I dialed the telephone number, and found that the puppies had been born and bred on a nearby farm in Sherifhales, Shropshire. The farmer's wife, Mrs. Jones, said it would be convenient for us to see the puppies that very afternoon.

Little Spotty in one of her cheeky moments.

Mom and I arrived at a busy, flourishing mixed farm run by Mr. Jones, his wife, and their teenage son. The terriers, in a kennel behind the house, barked excitedly when we arrived. In one run, there was a female and her four black and white puppies. They looked fat and healthy, but rather small for their age. I questioned Mr. Jones, but he insisted that they were all eating very well and were ready to go to their new homes.

I sat on the ground and began to play with the cute, very energetic puppies. I was drawn to one female, who had a white body, a black patch at the base of her tail, and a black patch over her right eye. She was smaller than the others, but sweet and mischievous. I scooped her up in my arms and she licked me gently on my cheek. I knew she was the one I wanted. I bought her for six guineas.

Spotty was the name I chose for her, after my original terrier. She traveled well on the flight over to America, snuggled in a cage I had made myself at the farm. Arriving back home, I opened the cage door to let her out and was surprised at how she ran out full of fun and energy despite her long journey. She was so tiny she stumbled over the grass, but as soon as she saw Rocky, who was waiting for me with Bob, she gathered herself together and ran over to him as fast as her little legs would carry her. It was love at first sight for both of them.

At nights she would snuggle right down underneath the bed covers, burrowing until she had chosen a cozy position in which to sleep. Early in the morning she would sleepily emerge, wagging her short tail, with many licks for Bob, Rocky, and myself.

Little Spotty was small enough for me to gather in my arms and hug. The bond between the two of us was like no other.

Chapter 15

Fursman Kennels

After the benefit for Mrs. Costello, I lost all feeling and respect for Bob. I seemed to be on a one-way train ride going nowhere. My unhappiness added to my restlessness. I wouldn't have minded working so hard and having no money if there had been love, but that wasn't so. Without Rocky and Spotty, my life would have been empty and insignificant. I didn't feel like a wife and couldn't foresee any change in the future.

A small, furnished house was for rent in Middleburg at a reasonable price, so I decided to move there until I had made up my mind exactly what I was going to do. I loved Middleburg, and one idea I had seriously considered, in view of my past experience, was to open a boarding kennel, if I could find suitable property.

Through Bob's training her racehorses, I had made friends with Jane Gunnell, a dark-haired lady with two small children. I happened to mention to her that I was looking for a place to open a kennel for dogs and cats. To my surprise she responded immediately and enthusiastically, "My father owns property in Middleburg; it would be the perfect spot for a kennel. I can take you there now."

You can imagine how excited I was as I climbed into her car heading towards what I hoped would be an ideal place for my new venture.

Turning off Route 50, one mile west of Middleburg, we drove down a long, unkempt lane, finally arriving at what was nothing more than a junkyard. This was a complete surprise to Jane; she apparently had no idea that the property was in such appalling condition. I felt heavy-hearted and crestfallen as we stood in an area covered with all kinds of rubbish: abandoned cars, farm equipment, beer cans, empty bottles, overgrown grass, and bramble bushes.

Carefully stepping over the rubbish, looking out for snakes, we approached a very old, dirty stable. On opening the doors of the stalls we found that they too were filled with trash.

Looking very embarrassed, Jane said, "Come on, Pam, let's go, you don't want this place." We left and I felt a bitter disappointment as we drove away. However, sitting at home I couldn't get Mr. Gunnell's property out of my mind. I decided I could not rest until I had gone back on my own and looked at it one more time.

As I stood a second time amid the rubbish, the old horse barn, and two old deserted houses, my thoughts and feelings began to be quite different from those of my first visit. The place did have some possibilities. There were huge, ancient oak trees towering overhead, as well as other smaller dogwood trees and shrubs that could be salvaged from the encroaching scrubby undergrowth. It was awful to think how the previous tenants had abused the property. I learned later that it had become a late-night hangout for people who parked there to drink.

Given half a chance, this piece of property could be made beautiful. I gazed up at the branches of the oaks swaying gently in the breeze. They gave me a feeling of serenity I hadn't experienced in a long time.

I felt that here was a challenge I just had to confront. It would be a tremendous undertaking, but somehow I felt certain that I could master it. Without giving myself a chance to reconsider my decision, I drove to see Mr. Gunnell, a man I had never met. Luckily, I found him at home and introduced myself as a friend of his daughter, Jane.

I came straight to the point and asked him if he would rent me the place with the old horse barn. A warm smile came over his face as he asked, "Do you really want to rent that barn, Pam?" I explained to him that I had owned and managed a successful kennel in England, and that I thought I could make a go of it in this area. Bruce Gunnell looked at the floor and, with his foot, moved his collie dog's bed nearer to the wall. "All right, Pam, you can have it," he said.

Taking a deep breath, I said, "Mr. Gunnell, how much rent do you want?"

He paused for a moment, and then with a twinkle in his eyes said, "How about $50 per month?"

I couldn't believe how little he wanted, but as this was a professional proposition, I replied that I would have to do a tremendous amount of work to make the property suitable to open a kennel. Hesitating a little, I then said, "How about $30 per month?"

Without further ado, he stretched out his hand and took mine in a firm handshake. The deal was made. The property was now mine, at least for the time being.

The next major hurdle was to secure a license from Fauquier County to operate my kennel. I had been warned by several dog owners that this would be very difficult to obtain, particularly since the property was on the edge of Middleburg and smack in the middle of an area of large horse farms.

I held my breath for the three-week period that the county required me to publish notices in the local newspapers, giving people a chance to comment on my pending venture. The time seemed an eternity, but thank goodness no one complained.

The next hurdle was my hearing before the county Board of Supervisors in Warrenton. The board members asked all kinds of questions: how long had I been around dogs, exactly what experience had I had, what were my intentions concerning the kennels? Finally, it was time for them to vote. What a relief-they were all in my favor. Now I was ready to get down to work.

The money Rocky and I earned during the three-day supermarket convention ($300 plus expenses) enabled me to get started with what was going to be a very expensive venture.

You will remember that I came over to America with only fifty pounds in my pockets, and during the two years before I was married I had saved $2,000. But since I didn't have an income during the years I was married to Bob, I spent what little money I had on food, petrol, and clothing. I began to focus my life around Rocky, Spotty, and my new business venture. The barn structure was sound-it had six stalls and a tack room-and I decided it would be my first project. Luckily the previous tenants had left a wheelbarrow, which made it easier for me to clean the deep manure from out of the stalls and barrow it up into the woods. For some reason old broken snow fences were piled in the tack room. I jostled and struggled to get each one onto the wheelbarrow and pushed them a good distance away from my soon-to-be kennels. Having accomplished that, I could see what I was up against inside the building.

Cobwebs were hanging from the ceiling, full of big black spiders and flies which had gotten tangled in the webs. Armed with a broom (also left behind) and wearing old clothes, a head scarf, and cotton gloves, I went into action, madly swinging in all directions, attacking the very much-at-home cobwebs until every one lay on the floor. What a dirty job, as the tangly webs dropped on my face and into my eyes.

The dirt on the floor was happened to be perfectly level and fine for me to lay concrete; this was a task I had never done before, but I had seen it done several times and luckily had paid attention.

I bought ready-mix concrete in bags, a shovel, and a trowel, and found a six-foot two-by-four lying in the woods. I mixed the cement little by little, in my wheelbarrow, and slowly but surely laid it in position on the floor, leveling it with my piece of wood and smoothing it with the trowel. The whole procedure took me seven days. It was strenuous work, particularly getting the floor level.

The next step was to build the kennels out of chainlink fence. I made them in sections approximately six by twelve feet, which made it easier for me to install them.

The interior of the barn needed to be painted. In the old days in England the farmers would mix lime, water, and a little cement to use as paint; it was cheap and it made a good job for this purpose as well. It wasn't that I was penny-pinching, I just didn't have the money to spare-and, besides, it looked just as good as expensive paint.

The outside of the kennels had never been painted, so I decided to do exactly the same as I did on the interior. My method would probably stay white for at least five years, but it needed two coats. I scraped the windows and doors and painted them a rustic red. The combination went well together and gave the appearance of a clean, well-kept kennel.

The dogs needed to be exercised while in my care, so my next project was to clear the immediate area around the kennel. Picking up the rubbish was an appalling job. I had to be very careful because I didn't know what might be lurking among the heaps of filth and dirt. Wearing thick gloves, I gradually gathered everything together and, with my wheelbarrow, trundled it into a huge unsightly pile at one end of the property.

After laboriously building my mountain of trash, I called Mr. Grayson, the local garbage collector, to bring his large truck and take it all away. Bob Sharp, whom I met through Rocky when he gave a performance at the Hill School, which

Bob's son John attended, drove to the kennels with his bulldozer and dug huge pits on the property to bury the heavy rusting iron of abandoned farm machinery. He also bushhogged the densely overgrown brush, grass, and weeds. Finally, with great relief, I arranged to have the abandoned cars taken away.

Now I could build runs big enough for the dogs to run and play. I made them very secure, putting nine-foot posts three feet into the ground and stretching chainlink fencing between each post. The gates I bought were strong, so there would be no chance of dogs escaping.

Everything was completed in two months of working long, hard hours. My style, as taught by my father, was to be 100 percent, and for me, it made sense to work very efficiently. I had saved literally thousands of dollars (which I didn't have) doing the work myself. Despite the money Rocky had earned for me, I had very limited funds to invest in my new enterprise. Amazingly, I was really enjoying myself, and it gave me great satisfaction to create a beautiful kennel from a place that previously had been a complete shambles.

I felt so proud of what I had achieved, and I was now ready to put an advertisement in the paper to let people know I was open for business. The name I had chosen for my business was Fursman Kennels, which was my father's middle name and my grandmother's maiden name.

The advertisement read: "Rocky, who has just returned from a promotional tour in Houston, Texas, wishes to announce the opening of a boarding and training kennel in Middleburg, Virginia. Please call . . ."

I always knew that the overwhelming response was due to Rocky's fame. Clients came from all over Loudoun and Fauquier counties to have their dogs boarded or trained for short or long periods of time. In a very short time the kennel had become a thriving business, enabling me to hire another person to work in the kennel as my assistant.

Over the next several years I was kept very busy continually improving and expanding the kennels and enjoying taking Rocky to his various performances. By this time the kennels were very successful. I was still renting and began to worry about not owning the property.

I had spent so much time, effort, and money, yet had no guarantee that all I had accomplished would remain mine. I knew I was taking a tremendous risk investing thousands of dollars in someone else's property, but it was very necessary to have a clean, respectable appearance. Dogs were now being brought by their owners from all over the country to visit my sanctuary for dogs and cats.

My own wants were very simple, just the everyday house expenses, so I was able to save more than $80,000 over the years, with the hope of buying the nearly seven acres of property.

I had come to know my landlord, Mr. Gunnell, quite well, as he used to come by every so often to see how things were progressing. I had already tried to buy the property from him, to no avail. The reason Mr. Gunnell hesitated selling me the property was that my rent was only $30 per month, and he thought it foolish of me to want to spend a lot of money buying land when my rent was so cheap. You see, Bruce Gunnell was one of those rare people for whom his handshake was his word and bond. But my anxiety continued to grow, and I decided to get up courage once again and ask if he would sell me the property.

One morning when I went into Middleburg to pick up my mail, I ran into Mr. Gunnell. We exchanged greetings and, as always, a handshake. I looked him straight in the eyes and said, "Mr. Gunnell, will you accept $10,000 per acre?" He looked taken aback, but with a smile on his face, and still holding my hand, he said, "Yes, Pam, I will sell it to you."

I could not contain myself and threw my arms around his neck and gave him a kiss on the cheek, right in the middle of the post office. A few days later, Mr. Gunnell came to the kennel to talk business, and very soon thereafter the property was mine.

Fursman Cottage with its English garden.

Chapter 16

Fursman Cottage

The excitement that night made it very difficult for me to sleep. My dreams of owning the property had finally come true. Now I would be able to put more of my architectural plans into motion and create a little bit of Staffordshire right on the edge of Middleburg. The old building to the right of the kennels was beyond repair, but the other one in the woods could be made into a real English cottage.

My personal life after leaving Bob was very difficult. The six years had taken more out of me than I had realized, my self-esteem was very low, and my nerves were so bad I was stuttering. I became a patient of Dr. Robert McConnell, who had a family practice in Middleburg. He helped me through this bad period of my life and a year later I divorced Bob.

At last I could foresee a move from the townhouse in Middleburg into my own dream cottage, and, what made it more exciting, I could create exactly what I wanted, using my own plans.

The day after talking to Mr. Gunnell I walked from the kennels over to the cottage to look it over thoroughly once more. Rocky, as usual, was by my side sniffing the fresh scent of the rabbits while little Spotty trotted behind, playfully nibbling on his tail.

The cottage had been empty for years. Windows and doors had been broken and vandalized. Luckily the tin roof was in good shape so water hadn't spoiled the old wooden floors, but over the years dampness had done a lot of damage. Some of the thick oak logs in the weakening walls were being eaten away by termites. Swallows had built their mud nests in the rafters, and small finches had theirs comfortably wedged in the old kerosene heater. Spotty surprised a snake as it hurriedly slithered back in its safe, dark hole.

I looked very carefully as I crept up the steep, narrow staircase. Situated at the top on the left was a small room with a slanted roof. To my immediate right, in a slightly smaller area, a glimmer of light was shining through a crack in the wood. I peeked through a tiny hole and could see sunlight shining through a broken window, and behind the divider, on the floor, was a huge pile of smelly old clothes and rubbish. I shook my head in disbelief and wondered what little creature had made a nest in what it thought was a wondrous find, in a dwelling that had been its home for years.

There were telltale holes on the the cottage where a groundhog had burrowed beneath the base of the building. Two sides of the cottage were stucco and in pretty good shape, but on the other sides there were oak logs, which had seen better days and were half rotted by the rain and termites.

Two doors led into the cottage-the one room had been the kitchen, the other a downstairs bedroom. Littered outside was the same kind of rubbish and old cars that had been over at the kennels. Near the doors, a huge oak tree once stood. It was over two hundred years old, but had recently fallen, breaking off at the roots. Luckily, it fell away from the cottage. The removal of the dead tree and the rubbish, and the remodeling of the cottage, were going to be a major, expensive project. The next day I happily drove to Warrenton to get permits for remodeling and drilling a well.

Charles Smith, a local builder who was very experienced in remodeling old houses, was recommended to work on my cottage. Mr. Smith and I had a good rapport. I would describe how I wanted each room to look, and fortunately he had a good imagination, so we often combined our thoughts and ideas.

Today the cottage looks as if it has been there forever, complete with low raftered ceilings and leaded window panes (which I hand-carried over from England). Looking out of the bay window in my sitting room, I enjoy a lovely view of the property.

A collection of David Winter's tiny cottages, given to me by different members of my family, adorns the windowsill. Next to the kitchen, with its tiled floor and raised-hearth fireplace, is a dining room decorated with oil paintings and Staffordshire china ornaments I have bought over the years. My bedroom downstairs looks out over the kennels, and a narrow staircase off the kitchen leads to a guest bedroom and bathroom. The interior of the cottage is cozy and has a warm, inviting feeling. The furniture is 18th-century style. After the surrounding outside area was cleared, I planted my favorite shrubs of rhododendrons, azaleas, and climbing roses. Crazy-paving footpaths lead to my front and back doors from the circle in front of my cottage in which I park my car.

Looking through my window, it is difficult to believe I am sitting in my own little cottage. The majority of the physical hard work is behind me, and everything that has been built or remodeled has been paid for.

My driveway leading off Route 50 was very dangerous, as it is a main highway with frighteningly fast traffic. I was always concerned that a client might have an accident coming into the kennels or when leaving. Three years after completing my cottage, I designed a gravel driveway from a side road just a short distance away from Route 50. It follows the contours of the rolling farmland leading into my property.

The new lane winding its way back to the kennels.

Rocky's grave.
I like to think he is watching everything that happens.

Chapter 17

Goodbye, Rocky

My dear Rocky had accomplished so many remarkable things over the years. The time had arrived when he deserved to enjoy a well-earned retirement. What fun we had walking over the fields and down the bridle paths leading into the woods. Together, we often visited Rocky's favorite pond. There he would sometimes swim for at least twenty minutes, every so often glancing my way to see if Spotty and I were watching him from the embankment.

From the beginning of Rocky's career, he had thrilled thousands of spectators at exhibitions in public and private schools throughout the country. Among his many performances were presentations at the Easter Seal Camp in Roanoke, the Pack 966 Cub Scout meeting held at the Sterling School in Virginia, and a very special exhibition for children in his own hometown at the Community Center in Middleburg.

As always, Rocky slept by the side of my bed. Every morning he would wake me up by touching me softly on the cheek with his wet nose. One morning, early in December 1976, he woke me up as usual, but that particular day he was whining softly. Leaning over the edge of my bed, I could see he

As you can see by the expression on Blakely's face,
Rocky had a special way with timid children.

was favoring his right front leg. I quickly jumped out of bed to examine him but could see no obvious signs of injury. I gently ran my fingers up his leg, and when I touched his shoulder he winced with pain. He turned his face to gaze at me with such sorrowful eyes, a look I had never seen before. I knelt by his side and put my arms around his neck, telling him everything was going to be fine.

Slowly I helped Rocky walk down the staircase. I dialed Dr. Rokus's number, keeping my fingers crossed that he would answer his phone at 6:30 in the morning. After only three rings Dr. Rokus answered. I explained to him that during the night pain had come into Rocky's shoulder, and before I could finish my sentence, he said, "Pam, bring him right now." Within fifteen minutes I was at the clinic. Dr. Rokus had switched on the lights and was waiting for us at his front door. "Bring him into the surgery, Pam," he said, in a concerned voice as he cast his eyes over Rocky. "Let's lift him up on the table."

Bill Rokus is a big, burly man with huge hands. To look at them you would never believe they were capable of performing intricate operations on animals. We carefully lifted Rocky onto the table and laid him on his left side. I stood stroking his head while he was being examined. "I need to x-ray him," Dr. Rokus said.

To my horror, the x-ray showed a mass of lesions on Rocky's lungs. The cancer was too far advanced for an operation. Dr. Rokus put him on analgesic pain pills and steroids to keep him as comfortable as possible at home.

I found it very difficult to accept that my beloved Rocky was enduring this terrible cancer. I had always been extremely careful regarding his food and diet. He had never been exposed to any chemicals and had always had plenty of fresh air.

During the next several weeks Rocky seemed like his old self. The lameness disappeared and his appetite was good. The medicine I gave him every twelve hours appeared to be keeping the cancer under control.

On December 20, Rocky was very quiet and didn't want to eat his breakfast. I called Joan, my assistant at the kennels, and asked her to run things because I wouldn't be coming to work for the next few days. I wanted to spend my time with Rocky.

His health deteriorated rapidly. I cooked him chicken and rice, hand feeding him at short intervals to try to sustain his strength, and repeatedly offered him water from a dish. He spent his last hours in the sitting room, lying on his bed next to my settee with Spotty snuggled up against his chest. I felt so helpless. My heart was breaking. I sat on the floor next to him with his head nestled on my lap. I tenderly stroked his forehead, trying to soothe his pain. I tried to put myself in his place. If I were very ill, I would want to have peace and quiet and not be disturbed, as the slightest movement, in his condition, took away all his strength. Little Spotty sensed there was something terribly wrong with Rocky, and she would lick him on his nose as she lay anxiously by his side.

Rocky was very brave during his short illness, and on December 23 he died peacefully with his head resting on my lap. If he had lived, he would have been nine years old January 4,

1977. Losing Rocky was devastating. I cannot express the emptiness and the hurt within my whole being. We had spent nearly nine years of our lives together, and most of that time had been twenty-four hours a day. My loneliness was like nothing I had ever experienced before. It was like losing my child, one I had loved and cherished since a baby. If a person has not gone through the tragedy of losing a pet, it must be difficult for them to understand why those of us who have grieve so deeply. Rocky's devotion had helped me through an unhappy marriage, and at his performances he was able to take children who were full of anger, especially teenagers, and turn it into joy.

After Rocky passed away, Spotty wandered endlessly around the house, searching and sniffing for her best friend. She would go to the front door asking to be let out, hoping she would find Rocky stretched out, relaxing on the grass, enjoying the sunshine as he had done for so many years. Spotty pined for Rocky about seven days and eventually seemed to accept the fact that he was never coming back. I buried Rocky in the flower bed next to the office, beneath the oak tree where he had often dozed in the languid summer afternoons.

On a warm night at the end of March, I needed to check on an older dog in the kennels around midnight. Returning to my cottage, as I passed the flower bed where Rocky was buried, I heard a strange cracking noise coming from the direction of his grave. I walked slowly to the flower bed and nervously bent over to have a closer look.

In the glow of the soft moonlight, to my amazement, I saw hundreds of daffodil shoots had burst up through the soil and realized that the sound I had heard was the force of the shoots cracking up through the earth by Rocky's grave.

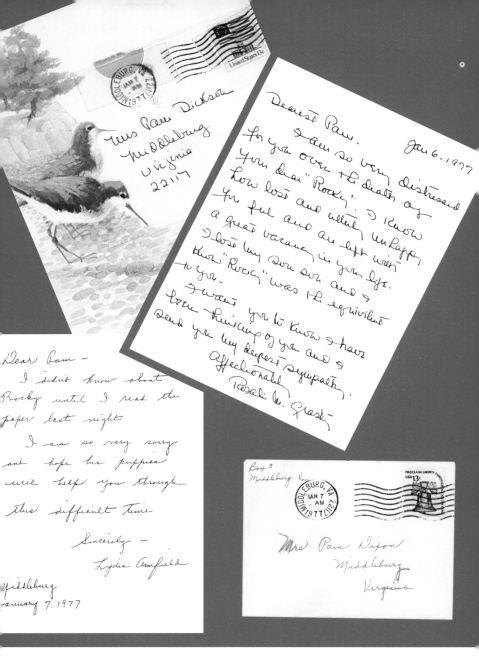

Dearest Pam.   Jan 6 - 1977

I am so very distressed
for you over the death of
your dear "Rocky". I know
how lost and utterly unhappy
you feel and are left with
a great vacancy in your life.
I lost my own son and I
know "Rocky" was the equivalent
to you.

I want you to know I have
been thinking of you and I
send you my deepest sympathy.
Affectionately

Rosalie M. Grast —

Mrs Pam Dickson
Middleburg
Virginia
22117

Dear Pam —
I didn't know about
Rocky until I read the
paper last night

I am so very sorry
and hope his puppies
will help you through
this difficult time

Sincerely —
Lydia Armfield

Middleburg
January 7. 1977

Box 3
Middleburg, Va.

Mrs. Pam Dixon
Middleburg
Virginia

Letters of condolence.

(165)

Emily North King riding Cobweb
after kindergarten when she was four years old.

Chapter 18

Middleburg Tales

I will always be grateful to Joan for taking care of the kennels during Rocky's last days. Finding and training good assistants has been essential to building my business. I can't do everything myself, as over the years it has grown considerably. I need people who are loyal to me and the animals, and who are willing to learn to do things my way. I also want to be able to give my staff responsibility and freedom, so they can perform with confidence on their own.

Running a boarding kennel is a seven-days-and-nights-a-week job, and it is more of a challenge than people could ever imagine. Even the person answering the phone is very important, as it gives a first impression to a client who is deciding whether to leave a pet with us. If the staff member has a caring voice, the owner is more likely to trust us.

I have always thought that our pets have feelings and emotions very much like our own. The only difference between us is that they cannot talk in our language. Animals do have a voice, whether it is a purr from a cat or a bark from a dog. Every species has a positive way of communicating with each other.

Dogs have an uncanny way of speaking with their eyes. Sometimes they are happy and vibrant, while if they get upset they can look very sad and downhearted. Stress can be common and can cause various kinds of illnesses. I have even heard of dogs losing their appetites and pining away when their mistresses or masters have died. Postoperative periods can be traumatic for them, and they need to be nursed back to health exactly as if they were human beings, with love and compassion.

As you can see, it takes a very special kind of person to work in a dog kennel, as the work is very strenuous and repetitive. A kennel worker's personality has to be happy and loving to owners who are sometimes very distressed at having to leave their loved ones, particularly if the animals need very special attention. The staff also has to be good with young dogs who are full of devilment and try to outwit their handlers, or sometimes insist on barking even when they are lying down on a feather bed.

"Jennifer," I said one day, glancing over at the dogs in their runs, "tomorrow Mrs. Emily North King will be bringing her three dogs to board for a few days, and she would like them to be bathed while they're here."

To take the edge off my assistants' jobs, I often tell them interesting stories about our clients. Now I told Emily's story to Jennifer.

Emily was born and raised in Warrenton. She had always been an animal lover, especially horses and dogs. At the age of four, she had managed to save three dollars pocket money to buy Cobweb, a thirty-nine-inch-high black pony. "She was a real little monkey," Emily told me. On one particular day, Emily's father and his camera caught Emily and Cobweb flying over a post and rail fence. Cobweb had obviously jumped too early, knocking down the top rail. Emily had landed on the pony's back behind the saddle, with arms and legs flailing wildly. The amusing photo of this incident is on a shelf in Emily's house.

As a teenager, Emily was an avid fox hunter, and in 1931, she rode in the first point-to-point organized by the Warrenton Hunt. The race covered eight miles across country which she knew well, beginning at Jefferson and finishing at Clovelly Farm. The flag went down for the start of the race, which was open to both men and women. Emily and her mount, Fireworks, a bay gelding, were off to a good start. The course took the riders over stone walls and board fencing, through fields and streams and between trees and bushes. Some of the trees had poison ivy lacing itself around the trunks and branches. Concealed groundhog holes made it crucial to watch the terrain of the course closely.

Fireworks was galloping along taking everything that came before him in stride. Then, rounding a bend on a deer track, they came upon a hidden strand of barbed wire. The horse came to a sliding stop as the sudden thrust and jolt of the wire hit his body forcefully across the chest. His head and body reared in the air. Emily, although secure in her saddle, immediately jumped off to see how badly the horse was hurt. Patting him gently, she noticed a slight bleeding cut on his chest. She quickly recalled a tip some gypsies had told her many years earlier. She gathered some old moist, dead leaves and packed them on the wound to stop the bleeding. After a few minutes the bleeding stopped, and Fireworks seemed none the worse for wear. Emily remounted, and even though they had been held up by the accident, they finished the race in third place.

"Wasn't that something?" Jennifer said with a look of admiration for Mrs. North King.

Now I couldn't resist telling a few more stories.

Another client is Mrs. Rosalie Grasty, who owns four miniature poodles named Baby, Killer, Mickey, and Heidi. Rosalie's ancestors came from Normandy. In 1066 the family moved to England during the reign of William the Conqueror. In 1623 the family had a falling-out with King James I, and they sailed to the New World, landing in Virginia. Rosalie was born in Charleston, South Carolina, the "cultural center of the South," where her father was in the lumber business. Her debut, held when she was eighteen years old, took place in Charleston, with over four hundred guests invited.

Rosalie's grandmother lived in Middleburg, Virginia. On one occasion, when she was visiting her, Rosalie met and fell in love with Frank Littleton. They married when Rosalie was twenty-one, and they settled down happily in the stone house Frank bought for his bride.

They both loved to entertain. At one of their brunches, they ran out of ice. It was an exceedingly hot day, and they didn't have a container large enough for the amount of ice they needed. So they quickly and thoroughly washed out the coal scuttle and went across the road to borrow ice from the undertakers. The brunch went on longer than they expected, so they made a second trip to the undertaker to ask for more ice. As Rosalie was standing in the entrance hall, a high-pitched voice shouted over the balcony. "Norees! Norees! If you give those people any more ice, that body won't last 'til Monday!"

When I told her this story, Jennifer nearly fell over on the floor laughing as tears rolled down her cheeks. So I went on to tell about an aristocratic older lady who lived in an elegant home several miles away from Middleburg. The lady had invited some friends, including Rosalie, in for a dinner party. The cocktails seemed to go on forever. Finally, the English butler came into the drawing room and quietly announced to the hostess, "Madam, dinner is served . . . but the cook is dead." No one believed him. Rosalie and several other guests went to the kitchen. There she was, lying flat on the kitchen floor, in Rosalie's words, "long gone dead." In true English style, the butler (keeping a stiff upper lip) was determined that the show must go on regardless. He had cooked the dinner himself. Needless to say, no one was hungry that night.

Jennifer's eyes grew large as I told yet another tale about the old theater in Middleburg. The locals went there to watch films on Friday and Saturday evenings. One night, a very old country man was sitting near the front. He had never seen a film before. During a scene when a train was coming straight towards the audience, the old man stood up and shouted hysterically, "You damn fools! You can stay here and get run over if you want to, but I'm leaving!" And he ran out of the theater.

These wonderful stories I told Jennifer were told to me by Rosalie one evening when I was having dinner at her home. Petite and elegant, with lovely silver hair, Rosalie took a sip of wine from her glass and told the next one. On the other side of Upperville, Virginia, there was a gorgeous old house, the home of an elderly lady. One night the butler entered the drawing room and announced to the invited guests that dinner was served, then assisted the old lady to the dining room. After dinner, the butler escorted her back to the drawing room and settled her in her armchair. She promptly dozed off. Presently, she awoke and pressed her bell for the butler. When he entered the room, she said to him, "John, you may serve dinner now." The butler replied that dinner had already been served. Whereupon the hostess replied irritably, "I don't recall it. Serve it again."

Fluffing the flowered pillow on her chair, Rosalie continued about a close friend of hers named Josephine. The friend organized a fancy dinner party, and one of her guests had too much to drink. He passed out in his chair. As a joke, Josephine called the undertaker to bring the hearse. Giggling, several of Josephine's friends, including Rosalie, loaded the drunken man into the hearse, covering him with flowers. Imagine his horror when he came around and realized where he was lying!

I was so entertained by Rosalie's tales that I hardly touched my drink. Reaching for a potato chip, I anxiously awaited the next yarn. We adjourned to the kitchen, since Rosalie suggested it was time to eat. As she filled my plate with steak, a baked potato and salad, she asked, with a gleam in her eye, "Have I told you about my contact lenses?" "No," I replied, wondering what on earth she was going to say next. With a slightly embarrassed look, she began:

"My gentleman friend and I were sitting on my terrace drinking champagne, chatting and admiring the view of the lovely Blue Ridge Mountains. The evening was drawing to a close. It had been a sultry and tiring day, and my eyes ached. So, I took out my contact lenses and dropped them into his nearby empty glass.

"We had finished the bottle and, relaxed and happy, we continued talking quietly. After a while, he asked if I had any more champagne on ice. As it happened, I did have another bottle in the fridge. After getting up to fetch it, I returned and gave the bottle to him to uncork. He filled both glasses with the frothy champagne, and we made another toast to each other. Later, when I remembered what I had done, I did not dare tell him that he had swallowed my contact lenses!

"At the end of the evening, after we had said our good nights, he left for home. I had just gotten into bed when the phone rang. My friend asked, 'Have you seen my shoes?' 'No,' I replied with amusement, 'I have not seen your shoes.' The next morning when I awoke, looking out of my bedroom window, I saw my handyman, William, looking at a pair of shoes on the terrace. Puzzled, he shook his head, then walked over to the terrace wall and peeked over it to see if anyone was on the other side. Then he picked up the offending shoes and carried them into the house. He placed them one in front of the other at the foot of the stairs. Lily, the maid, happened to see what he was doing and said, 'William, why have you placed the shoes like that?' 'Just in case there's a gentleman upstairs,' he solemnly replied. 'I don't want him to break his stride leaving!' "

"I can imagine everything clearly, can't you Jennifer?" I said. "What came next?" Jennifer inquired with much interest.

Well, after supper, we returned to the study and, settling into her big chair, Rosalie heaved a big sigh. Now, looking more serious, she told me that last December, Dudley and Cissy Bunn were hosting a party for the Middleburg Pink Box docents at seven o'clock. Most of the guests had already arrived when the telephone rang. Dudley, who happened to be standing nearby, answered the call. Mrs. Jean Gold, a longtime friend and world traveling companion of Rosalie's, was on the other end and said, "Hello, Dudley. Rosalie and I will not be coming to the party." "Oh, I'm so sorry," answered Dudley. "What is the problem?" Jean replied in a matter-of-fact voice, "Our car got stuck on the railroad and a train came along and totally demolished it. But don't worry, everything's now under control."

Rosalie explained that on the afternoon of the party, she and Jean had been Christmas shopping for their grandchildren. It was a dark, wintry evening. Jean was driving her car and, approaching the lane to the Bunns' home in Delaplane, Virginia, she mistakenly turned onto the railroad tracks, which ran parallel to the lane. Jean frantically tried to maneuver her car off the track, with the car's wheels spinning uselessly and the engine roaring. As moments ticked by, Jean realized she was not going to be able to move her car without help.

Fortunately for them, Mrs. Payne, who lived in a brick house near the railroad track, heard the screech of the spinning wheels and the frenzied grinding of the engine. She rushed outside shouting to them to get out of the car, as a train was due by in two minutes. They didn't hear her. So Mrs. Payne quickly sent her fourteen-year-old twin boys to warn the ladies, while she dialed the railroad to alert them. Jean and Rosalie immediately got out of the car when the boys warned them about the advancing train. Still in their high-heeled shoes, they scrambled down the embankment in the dark and darted across the lane up to the front door of Mrs. Payne's house.

Looking back, they saw the giant locomotive roaring along the track, crushing the car and tossing it in the air as though it were a shredded leaf. With sparks flying, the mile-and-a-half-long train with its four engines came to a gradual, grinding halt farther down the line. The engine driver had received the message too late to stop in time. With a twinkle in her eyes and lifting her glass, Rosalie said, "Now that was a close call! By the grace of God, someone was looking after us!"

Rosalie looked at me from her chair and asked, "Have you heard of Mosby?" "Yes," I said, I had heard of the brilliant Confederate leader and soldier who was in the Civil War. Keeping a straight face, I asked her if she was a Northerner. She faced me squarely and with fire in her eyes replied, "No, I'm not! I'm a Confederate!" She was so annoyed, I thought she was going to throw me out of her house! After she realized that I was only teasing her, she went on to tell me more about her ancestors.

Melmore House, located in Middleburg, had been in Rosalie's family for seven generations. Rosalie's great-grandmother, Anne, was married to George Adams and they had eleven children. During the Civil War there was much action in the Middleburg area. The local hero, Colonel John Mosby, was a lawyer from Warrenton who was also a good friend of Rosalie's great-grandparents. His military line of defense was "hit and run." In 1863, the Yankees were hot on his heels and Mosby, seeing the barn behind Melmore House, hid his horse and ran into the house. Mrs. Adams swiftly concealed the colonel in a secret attic room.

Not far behind him came the Yankee soldiers. They demanded that Mrs. Adams surrender Colonel Mosby. She responded that she didn't know what they were talking about. Pushing her aside, they forced their way into her home and made a thorough search for Mosby, convinced he was hiding there. Failing to find him, they told her to give him up or they would take her husband as a hostage. Mr. Adams was at home at the time recuperating from having lost a leg in the war. Besides taking her husband, the Union soldiers seized all the cows from the property. Several soldiers were left to guard the house. Finally, after three days they left, thus enabling Mosby at last to depart.

Mrs. Adams had been left with nothing to feed her large family. Desperately, she borrowed a neighbor's horse (Rosalie didn't know from whom). She rode through the firing lines to Fairfax to speak to Brigadier General Stoughton, a good-looking, dark-haired, bearded man about twenty-five years old.

Arriving at the enemy camp, she was escorted by a soldier to the general. She confronted him with the request to return her husband and cows. The general told her that he wanted Colonel Mosby. Mrs. Adams denied any knowledge of his whereabouts, saying he was no longer in Middleburg.

Fortunately for Mrs. Adams, the general was a true gentleman. He admired her bravery riding through the firing line and decided to return both her husband and her cows. From a nearby field, Mrs. Adams picked the number of cows stolen from her, selecting the ones with the largest udders, as she desperately needed the milk for her large family. She and her husband were escorted back to Middleburg, the soldiers helping to herd the cattle back into their field.

After I finished telling Rosalie's stories, I walked back towards my cottage, and Jennifer began taking dogs back into their kennels.

I thought for a moment about Rosalie's house. She had selected a site directly behind Melmore and across the road from the church cemetery and had built a home for her later years. Rosalie particularly liked the location, and her dry sense of humor showed through in the name she chose for her home.

"I say, Jennifer!" I shouted from over by the flower bed. "Would you like to know the name of Rosalie's house, which sits opposite the cemetery?" "What is it?" Jennifer replied. "En Route," I answered with a smile. Jennifer went into a fit of giggles as she continued to lead dogs back into the kennels.

Chip, the canine journalist.

Chapter 19

Chip's Tale

My name is Chip and, though I say so myself, I am rather good-looking, a light brown, long-haired terrier cross with a long tail, which I wag when I am happy. I am sixteen years old, but really very good-natured. I am fortunate to have always lived in a comfortable and loving home, and I am devoted to John and Jean, my master and mistress.

We have recently moved to the outskirts of Middleburg, where my owners bought a small horse farm in the beautiful Piedmont countryside overlooking the Blue Ridge Mountains. The old stone four-bedroom house is set in ten acres of paddocks, with a four-stall stable and tack room. John and Jean own two pleasure horses named Park Lane and Vision and are planning to go on cross-country rides and join the local hunt.

John has retired from a big law firm in Washington, D.C., and this is their retirement home, which we are all excited about. Each day brings me new and exciting discoveries. I often find old bones buried and forgotten by previous inhabitants, and I definitely enjoy wandering around the garden, paddocks, and stable area.

We had not been settled long when, one morning at breakfast, I overheard John and Jean discussing a trip they would have to take to Maryland, to attend to some business. My heart sank: What were they going to do with me? I could not imagine that they would leave me on my own. We had been here such a short time, and I knew we didn't know of anyone who could look after me. During all of my sixteen years I had never spent a night without either one of my family. I was very upset at the thought that they might leave me on my own. Who would feed me? What would I do all day without my master and mistress?

Sipping her cup of coffee slowly, Jean looked down at me and said, "Chip, I am very sorry to have to do this, but we are going to have to leave you for a few days at Fursman Kennels." She claimed these kennels were highly recommended by the real estate lady who sold us the property, but that didn't ease my mind very much.

Jean picked up the phone and dialed the kennels. I walked over quietly in order to listen to the conversation. To my dismay, I heard that I was being booked into the kennels for four whole days. Jean assured the person on the other end of the phone that my vaccinations were all up to date and my records would be brought with me the following day. I felt betrayed and panic-stricken.

After Jean put down the receiver, she bent down and picked me up, holding me close in her arms. With tears in her eyes as she said, "Chip, I love you so much, I hate to leave you, but you are going to a lovely kennel where you will be happy."

(180)

Jean kissed me as she put me down on the floor. With my tail between my legs I crept into my bed under the kitchen table. Curled up in a tight ball, I lay and imagined a perfectly dreadful four days ahead of me.

The next morning dawned bright and clear. I hadn't slept very well and woke up early with an awful sinking feeling in my stomach. Both John and Jean talked about how worried they were leaving a dog my age in strange surroundings. And rightly so, I thought! Jean, who usually drove, brought the car up to the front door so John could put the suitcases into the trunk. Then we all got in, with me sitting in the back seat.

All I could see through the window were the tops of trees and a bright blue sky. Eventually we turned off the main road and seemed to be driving slowly down some kind of lane. I could hear dogs barking in the distance. By this time I was a nervous wreck and was shivering badly. I could not believe they were actually leaving me. I thought they loved me as much as I loved them.

The car came slowly to a halt outside the office, and Jean got out and opened the back door. I edged away from her to the far side of the seat, but she reached in and gathered me in her arms and lifted me out. I felt helpless as she carried me into the office. John came in with us and handed my health certificates to an efficient-looking young lady standing by the desk. She had sparkling blue eyes, and in a friendly manner introduced herself as Jennifer. Her hand seemed to reach out automatically to touch me, as she said, "Hello, Chip. How are you? Aren't you beautiful?" Of course I already knew that, but it was nice of her to say so. Jennifer looked over my records and then filled out my personal guest card. She listened carefully, gently stroking my back, while Jean told her all about me.

Some special food had been brought for me, as occasionally I have a weak stomach. As it was the first time I had been left in a kennel, Jean worried that I might pine and refuse to eat. That would serve them right if I lost weight during my stay, I thought crossly.

Meanwhile, I was becoming aware of mouth-watering smells. Glancing around, I noticed that the office was also a shop, stuffed full of the most exciting things imaginable-cans of food and packets of biscuits, treats in all shapes and sizes, collars, leads, brushes, comfortable beds, toys, chews, and great handmade coats.

"Would you like to get Chip a treat to eat while he stays with us?" Jennifer asked. Boy, oh boy, what luck! I was put on the floor and wandered around sniffing at all the doggie treats available. Finally, I chose lamb and rice biscuits, which smelled delicious even through the wrapping paper.

The office door opened, and in walked a young lady about seventeen years old with red hair and freckles on her face. Jennifer introduced us to Cathy and said she would be helping take care of me. As Cathy bent over and picked me up, I was surprised how gently she handled me. But I could see that John and Jean were feeling as sad as I was, as they said good-bye, waving as Cathy carried me into the kennels.

Cathy put me in one of the many large runs so that I could go to the bathroom if I needed to. I had not been in the run but a few minutes when Pam (the owner, I was to learn) came from out of the center door in the kennels towards me. A very friendly person, she petted me and said she was delighted to have me stay for a few days.

My exercise gave me the opportunity to have a good look around. I must say, everything was very clean and tidy. The runs were raked, the kennels freshly painted, and even the windows sparkled. There was a lot of activity going on in the kennels, and the phone rang off and on.

Cathy came out to my run and said, "Come on, Chip, it's time to come in," and she snapped the lead onto my collar and walked me into an enclosed veranda. Here I was surprised to see a double kitchen sink and neatly arranged cans of cat and dog meats on the shelves. The floor was covered with a soft grey carpet, which made the area look comfortable and cozy, and there were also feed bins and a refrigerator. To the right of the refrigerator, hanging on the wall, was a large blackboard with dogs' names on it, listing their own special food or medicine.

I was led into the section of the kennels where I would be staying. My kennel was spacious and secure, with a comfortable bed and a bowl filled with fresh water in one corner. I even had my personal outdoor run. Giving me a friendly pat, Cathy said, "Chippy, you are going to enjoy being here."

Once on my own, I climbed into my bed and sat and listened to the noises around me. Nice music was playing in the background, and a telephone was on a nearby table-great; I would be able to hear if my owners called. Cathy and Jennifer, chatting cheerfully, started to lead the other guests out into the runs for early-morning exercise. There was a lot of excited barking and wagging tails, and everyone had the chance to exchange sniffs or friendly growls through the wire. I was beginning to think this wasn't such a bad place after all.

While the other dogs were outside playing in the runs, I could see and hear Pam and her staff going through the kennels, first picking up the beds and water bowls, then hosing the kennels down and using bleach to freshen them. I could figure that out by the smell. Before putting down the beds and clean water bowls, the floors were hand-dried with towels. Once the carpets in front of the kennels were vacuumed, the doors and windows were dusted, which made everything spotless. It was time for the dogs to return to their kennels.

Since I had never expected to go to a kennel, I hadn't given a thought on how they were run. I was completely amazed. "Why", I thought to myself, "this place is cleaner than home."

Pam and Jennifer started to prepare our meal. "Me first, me first," everyone was saying with loud barks and wagging tails. We were served on different-sized dishes, according to our size and appetites. When it was my turn for my special food, I found I was hungry. Normally, I am a rather picky eater, but today I ate my food heartily and then licked the dish clean, pushing it around my kennel. Well, at least they won't have to do much cleaning up on my bowl, I thought.

In the meantime, Cathy was picking up droppings and hosing down the outside runs and spraying them. The cleanliness of the runs, I heard Pam say, is very essential to keep them free of disease.

After everyone had eaten breakfast, we were all taken out for playtime. I was put in a run near the kennels' entrance so I had a good view of what was going on around me. There were at least twenty large runs, with all breeds of dogs in them. Some were small; others were larger; each with its own personality. Some dogs were friendly, while others would glare at each other through the wire fence until they were reprimanded by Pam.

After a short walk, I felt quite contented to lie down comfortably and watch the busy activities. Dogs that were going home that day looked sleek and well groomed; their nails were clipped, and they were either brushed and combed or had been bathed and blow-dried.

I always believed I had been spoiled by John and Jean, until the amazing event that I am about to relate. About mid-morning the sound of wheels on the gravel drive grew louder; as the car came in view around the circle, we saw a very long, chic, black limousine glide elegantly to a stop directly in front of the office door. Everyone was curious to see what highly refined human being was about to step out of that humongous car. All ears were pricked with anticipation, as we watched a man dressed in a black uniform and wearing a peaked cap emerge from out of the driver's seat. He walked around the front of the limousine to the rear door, leaned slightly forward, and opened it.

What happened next was quite something. Instead of a dainty lady wearing high heels and a fashionable dress, out tumbled three white Bichon Frise dogs, followed by a maid wearing a white smock. The little dogs' legs carried them in all different directions. First they sniffed the office steps and then moved on to the next exciting smell, which led into the kennels where Cathy was waiting. She individually patted and welcomed each dog. Their names were Betsy, Teddy, and Wally.

In the meantime, the maid had gone into the office to see Jennifer, while the chauffeur opened the large trunk of the limousine and proceeded to take out three large beds and a picnic basket. Somehow he managed to gather all three beds under his left arm and carried the picnic basket in his right hand. He then walked with great difficulty into the kennels, finally heaving the items up onto a table. Having put Betsy, Teddy, and Wally into their kennels, Cathy walked over to the chauffeur to get the beds. Reaching over them, she opened the picnic basket. A broad smile came over her face as she looked up at him.

"Let me show you what Mrs. Joynt has sent with her three little angels," he said, lifting everything out of the basket onto the table. We could see that there were specially prepared individual packets of rice and chicken, to be given morning and evening. The chauffeur said the other packets were biscuits, to be given each day at twelve o'clock.

Then, without further ado, he touched his cap to Cathy and walked out of the kennels to his limousine. He waited a few minutes for the maid to come out of the office, then politely escorted her into the back seat and drove off down the lane, just as sedately as he had come. By now we all were quite speechless, not really believing our ears and eyes. But after a few seconds we all chatted amongst ourselves and were inspired by the thought that perhaps one day it could happen to us. I learned later that it was a regular thing for maids and limousine drivers to deliver the beloved pets of their owners!

Several owners drove up during the day to collect their dogs and were greeted with happy barks and joyful prancing. Obviously these dogs had enjoyed their visit at the kennels, but they were looking forward to going home. They leaped straight into their cars through the open door, and I heard snatches of conversation from the owners as they drove off down the drive. I was impressed when I heard that some of the dogs were owned by famous celebrities.

One arrival was particularly entertaining to watch. A pickup truck braked sharply as it stopped at the kennels, and four little terriers inside were all barking and jumping excitedly at the door window. The driver walked around the front of the truck, and when he opened the door all the terriers fell out together in a jumble on the drive. They quickly recovered, shook themselves, and then scampered into the kennels. Obviously they had stayed here before.

A few minutes later, while Jennifer was in the office, Ilene Hackman arrived. Pam happened to be looking out of the veranda window and saw her hurriedly get out of her car dragged by a strong and uncontrolled Jack Russell, who was pulling very hard on his lead. Foreseeing what might happen, Pam shouted, "Stay where you are and I will get Sunday." The lady shouted back, "That's all right, Pam, I can manage," but the tricolored terrier by this time had built up his strength and was really straining on his lead. Suddenly his owner lost her balance, fell backwards, and landed full-length on the ground, still clutching the lead.

With a horrified look, Pam raced out of the kennels to help the lady and get Sunday, who was still straining towards the gate. "Are you all right?" asked Pam.

"Yes, thank you, I'm fine," Mrs. Hackman said as she stumbled to her feet, "but I do feel a bit silly!"

Well, that's excitement for you, I thought, my eyes practically bulging out of my head with all I had seen in the past few minutes. Never a dull moment, that is for sure! I was beginning to think this was the place to spend a holiday.

Another service at the kennels was the photographs that Pam took of dogs and cats. I had noticed several of them hanging on the wall in the office. This morning a photographic session had been arranged by their owner for two golden retrievers.

They were brought out of their kennels, led by Cathy and Jennifer, each carrying a brush. The dogs, to me, seemed completely out of control, like young, unbroken horses, rearing and plunging as they were taken into a run. It was very obvious to me that none of them had ever been on the lead.

Pam joined them in the enclosure, which was covered with lush, green grass. Her camera was hanging around her neck, and in her hand was a squeaky toy. I heard Pam say, "Take the collars off from around their necks, so they'll look natural."

Wow, that was exactly what the retrievers wanted. When they were released, they raced around playing and pulling at each other's legs and tails, having a rare old time. After a while they settled down, and Cathy and Jennifer brushed their coats, making them look more presentable for the camera.

Pam wanted Peanut and Woody lying next to one another. That, I could see, would be a miracle in itself. To accomplish this, leads were put around their necks, and each dog was put in position. Then the leads were taken off and the handlers moved away. That was when chaos broke out. One dog rolled over with his feet in the air, and the other ran cheerily around the enclosure barking.

After they had been retrieved, each dog was once again brushed carefully and put back in position, leads taken off, and the handlers backed away cautiously. Quickly, Pam focused her camera, at the same time telling the dogs to "stay." I could hear the camera clicking rapidly, catching them before they decided to move. Cathy stood behind Pam squeezing the squeaky mouse to attract the dogs' attention-which to my surprise she succeeded in doing. Pam was able to take some natural shots of them lying together looking over the fields. "Fantastic! I think we have what I need," said Pam as she walked over to the studio.

A little later Jennifer lifted a dog up onto a table which stands underneath the kennel eaves and was brushing, combing, and talking to Daisy, a long-haired terrier. Pam and Cathy were bathing a large, difficult collie dog in the grooming salon.

A car drove up and parked by the office, and out climbed a young woman with two small dogs in her arms. Jennifer shouted to her, "Will you please come on in!" Appearing flustered as she opened the gate, clutching her little pets, the woman introduced herself as Linda Jones. She said she

Lassie

Buster & Cara

Terra

Gus

Gilly

Woody & Peanut

Daisy

Lily Bell

Huck & Lacy

*Portraits of my fellow guests,
all taken by Pam during their
holiday at Fursman Kennels.*

Foxy

had known Pam a long time and hadn't had a dog for several years, but now she had acquired these two little souls and would like to leave them at the kennels for a few days.

She seemed rather nervous at leaving them and was speaking in a low voice, which was making it rather difficult for me to hear. I moved my position to get as close to the fence as possible, with my best ear towards Jennifer and Linda, who said, "I would like to tell you about my little dogs, so you will understand and treat them very carefully."

Jennifer rested her hand on Daisy's neck as she listened intently to what Linda had to say.

In 1992, an elderly man lived in the Fort Lauderdale area with his two beloved dogs, Nicky, a female white Maltese, and Peanut, a male brown Shih Tzu. He had bought them both at eight weeks old, and life thereafter had been a lot less lonely. Looking after his dogs helped to pass the long days, and he enjoyed spoiling them: Nicky was even allowed to eat off the table!

But eventually, the old man became very ill with cancer and so hired a husband-and-wife team to take care of him, the dogs, and the house. The couple had been recommended by an agency, but unfortunately, neither of them cared for dogs. He was not aware of this until his neighbor, who saw them through the window, told him that his beloved pets were being mistreated. The husband was the worse bully, cursing at the dogs and hitting out at them. He would pull Nicky's ears in a temper, eventually damaging the nerves, and even struck her on her jaw so hard that he broke it.

(192)

Poor little Nicky and Peanut went from being happy and contented dogs to being timid and miserable animals. Peanut did try to protect Nicky by growling, but with such beastly human beings he had no chance to improve their circumstances. Linda's voice began to shake, but she carried on.

In October of 1992 Hurricane Andrew hit the east coast of Florida. In a terrifying moment the old man's house was badly damaged. Petrified by the howling winds and the devastation all around them, the dogs ran away. Days later the Fort Lauderdale Rescue Team found them huddled together under a fallen tree. After gentle coaxing, the two little dogs allowed themselves to be caught. Fortunately, they both had name tags on their collars, so the rescue team was able to contact their owner. The old man was brokenhearted and begged them to find a kind home together for his beloved friends. He was far too ill to be able to take care of them again.

Teresa Garcia was in charge of the Washington, D.C. adoption program and had placed an advertisement in the *Washington Post* asking for special homes for the orphan dogs of Hurricane Andrew. Linda, living in Middleburg, answered the advertisement, as she was looking for a small dog for her two little girls. In reply to her telephone inquiry, Miss Garcia said, "I have a small white female Maltese, but she has a little friend, and we very much want to get them both adopted together." Linda said she had plenty of room in the house and a lot of acreage and would love to give them both a good home.

Arrangements were made for both Nicky and Peanut to be flown up from Fort Lauderdale to Washington. On arrival the little dogs were very timid, especially when Linda's husband entered the room, but with time and plenty of love and patience from all of Linda's family, Nicky and Peanut are now coming along beautifully. They have learned to trust and love their new family. Only when a storm is coming do they now show fear: they seem to sense one in advance and run and hide under the couch. Peanut occasionally cries and twitches in his sleep, no doubt having a nightmare of those unpleasant days before and during Hurricane Andrew.

"So now you understand why I needed to talk, and for you to meet my little dogs," Linda said in a concerned voice.

I don't mind telling you, what I had just heard about my two distant cousins was very upsetting, and it made me realize how lucky I have been during my long life to have such wonderful owners. Jennifer looked so sympathetic as she said good-bye to Peanut and Nicky, she promised to love and take good care of Linda's little dogs when they arrived next week.

At the end of playtime, I noticed that Jennifer and Cathy took the noisier dogs in first. That meant, naturally, I was the last to be taken into my kennel. As Cathy carried me indoors, she kissed me on the top of my head. Being pampered, I found, helped make me feel more at home. I went straight to my bed, which I noticed had been fluffed up, and, to my delight, I found that one of my biscuits had been left for me as a surprise.

As I munched away on my biscuit, I could hear familiar sounds of last-minute preparation so everything would be immaculate for the afternoon.

Jody is a twenty-year-old young man, with a slim-built frame and fair hair. He is a cheery soul who genuinely seems to love dogs and cats. It is he who takes charge in the afternoons. I noticed that the first thing Jody did when he arrived was to familiarize himself with the new boarders, read over the notes, and put any new bookings on the calendar. He then made out cards for new clients.

My first day I learned that midday was a rest period for all the boarders, unless collected by their owner. At about two o'clock we were taken, in turn, back out into the runs for exercise. If the weather was good, we were allowed to stay there a little longer. When my turn came, I was surprised to see different dogs from those in the morning. Obviously, they were staying in a section of the kennel I couldn't see. Some of them were much larger than me and looked rather intimidating, while others even smaller than me made me feel very superior. I soon decided to lie down, as I had done in the morning, and watch the various people coming and going.

After a few minutes, a maroon van drove up. I recognized the large, smiling man who got out as Willard Scott, the NBC TV weatherman. He opened the back door, and out tumbled three dogs, making their way straight to the entrance gate. They turned out to be Cara, a black Labrador; Buster, a cream collie; and Elvis, a shepherd-terrier cross. I overheard Pam telling Cathy that all three of these dogs had been abandoned up on the mountain, and the kindhearted Scotts had given them a wonderful, loving home. I heard Mr. Scott say to Jody, "Thank you very much, Mary will pick them up on the

15th." He started up the van, waving as he drove away just as another car arrived. In it was a frail elderly lady, with her tiny Yorkshire terrier, which couldn't have weighed much more than a pound. Very emotionally she handed him over to Jody, tears streaming down her cheeks as she tried to explain.

Toby was her baby, and she couldn't bear to be apart from him the next two days. She had brought Toby's little bed, and his toys. She said his favorite food was chicken, and she wondered if we would be able to prepare it for her tiny dog.

Jody was very kind and said to her, "Of course, we can cook it for Toby fresh each day in our microwave, and please don't worry. I promise we will look after him just as if he were our own child." I saw the lady put her arms around Jody as she turned away tearfully, looking back at Toby, then she climbed in her car and drove away.

Jody brought Toby in and put him in a smaller kennel in my section, the place where the smaller or older dogs seemed to be kept. I could hear him speaking to Toby as if he were a person, settling him in his own bed and giving him fresh water in a tiny bowl.

I don't mind telling you I had no idea the dogs would be treated with such individuality as they are at these kennels.

The back of the kennels are covered outdoor runs in case of bad weather. As I was relaxing, lazily watching Jody hose down the concrete floors, I noticed how the water ran down into a sloping shallow channel, gathering speed as it went. It was a warm day and the flowing water looked so inviting. Smiling to myself, I could imagine a young chipmunk having fun sitting

Kitty tantalizing the dogs.

(197)

on a leaf shouting "wheeee" as he slid down the 150-yard channel.

The afternoon was coming to an end, and Pam's cat was still in the garden. Jody suddenly let out a loud cry, "Kitty, kitty, kitty," looking out over the lawn. Within a short time, a tabby cat came running around the corner. It was time for her to be taken into the kennels for the night. Jody scooped her up in his arms, and they both disappeared into the kennels. From then on I was to see Kitty several times a day, as she loved to tantalize the dogs by jumping up on the high fence of one of the runs. The dogs in the runs took great delight in watching Kitty maneuver herself up onto the top rail of the fence, with her tail straight up. She thought she was very clever, and knew she was safe up there, giving her tightrope walker's performance. She would then jump down and walk proudly to the house, her tail held high.

As the sun went down and twilight dimmed, I could hear my fellow guests settling down for the night, the rustling of paws scratching a bed into a comfortable position, the occasional sleepy bark and quiet lapping of water from a drinking bowl. It had been a long, exciting day and I was very tired. So much had happened since morning that I had not had much time to miss John and Jean, but my last thoughts were of them. Later that evening I heard Pam quietly check on us all, and from then on I slept through the night, dreaming of my wonderful day at Fursman Kennels.

Chapter 20

Bigger and Better

To the right side of the kennels there was a fifteen-by-thirty-foot old, shabby building with a slanting roof, which the original farmer on the property used as a tractor shed. For several weeks I tossed ideas around in my mind about what to do with this big wooden structure. It was 1983, and the kennel business was doing well. During the winter months my boarders were just as plentiful as in the summer months. Virginia weather in the winter can be very unpredictable, which can make it very difficult for my staff to travel to work. I decided the logical and practical thing to do would be to remodel the building into a cottage, so a staff member could live on the property. The location was perfect: it had a beautiful view, overlooking the fields where my neighbor's horses grazed, and the five pine trees I had planted in between the oaks would make it very private, both for the tenant and for myself.

My plans were to make the main shed into a sitting room and kitchen, and then build a twelve-by-eighteen-foot bedroom with an adjoining bathroom. The rooms would have large airy windows, and the design would blend right into the landscape, transforming the old tractor shed into what looked like an old-fashioned wood cabin.

Within two months of commencement, everything was completed, right down to the painting and the fitted grey carpets covering the floor. It turned out to be a real asset to the property and looks as if it has been there forever.

About 300 yards to the left of my cottage stands an old hay barn with a good tin roof, where the farmer kept the hay for his cattle. But the large run-in shed that was attached to the hay barn had collapsed on the ground, leaving a huge pile of concrete posts, wooden beams, and tin roofing, none of which I could salvage.

I phoned my by-then good friend Bob Sharp to ask him to please come with his bulldozer and dispose of all the junk. It took him several hours to push it together and load it on a long-base truck and haul it away.

Fixing up the hay barn was a straightforward job. Charles Smith laid concrete on the base. On the sides of the barn we put sturdy old oak boards (which were in very good condition) from a large horse barn that was being taken down by a neighboring farmer, and its double doors were a perfect fit for my barn.

While I had Mr. Smith working on the property, I decided to build an adjoining two-stall horse stable and a small tack room. Directly in front of the stalls I designed an area in which a horse could be put on cross ties and groomed; beyond the cross ties we put a place for a carriage.

One thing led to another. If I was to buy a horse, I would have to have my property enclosed by board fencing and divided into two paddocks, which I did. Life is very funny. No sooner had I finished building the stable and fencing my paddocks than a friend told me there was going to be a horse sale nearby, where a donkey and her week-old baby were entered. The sale was the following Saturday starting at noon, and luckily the donkeys were to be sold early.

I don't know if you've ever noticed that all donkeys have a cross on their backs. I was taught as a child by my Sunday School teacher that God marked the donkeys at birth, after one had carried Mary to Bethlehem, where she gave birth to Jesus. They have a black line starting between their ears, running completely down the neck to the tail. An intersecting line runs across their shoulder blades, finishing halfway down the shoulders. These two lines form a complete cross.

The morning of the sale arrived. I was feeling very excited, just as I did when Dad and I went to the sale in England. I felt like a child again, as my mind flooded with memories of those wonderful days. The drive down the winding Zulla Road is one of serenity. Glancing over the fences, I could see horses and cows grazing in the paddocks with the Blue Ridge Mountains lying majestically in the distance. The sun was streaming through the delicate new leaves of the oak, maple, and poplar trees, and the magical white flower of the Virginia dogwood lined the hedgerows and woodlands. Years ago this road had been an old Indian footpath, leading to where I am not quite sure.

Within a few minutes I had arrived at the sale. It was difficult to find a parking spot for my car, as there were a lot of horse vans and trailers parked every which way in the front field. Entering the front door of the auction building I maneuvered my way through narrow passages filled with people chatting to each other about this horse and that pony. My emotions were kindled as I sidled in and around the crowd, looking anxiously in every stall for the donkeys. Finally I came to the stall where the donkey and her baby were. They both looked nervous and afraid. The mommy was grey in color and very much on the lean side, while her baby, who was lying down, looked healthy. He had very large ears and a light grey body with white markings—quite an unusual color for a donkey.

I was about to open the gate and walk inside the stall to pet them, when, without provocation, a huge brown horse in the next stall flew at the dividing partition and reached over, with his ears pinned back flat and his mouth wide open. He bared an enormous set of teeth and tried to bite the donkey and her baby. The mommy scurried out of his reach as the baby scrambled to his feet, falling against the partition in his haste to escape. Unscathed, he picked himself up and shakily huddled against his mommy, who was looking terrified.

I was appalled to have witnessed such a nasty drama and beckoned a staff person who happened to be nearby, asking him to please move the ill-tempered horse to a different stall, far away from those precious donkeys. Once he was removed, I went into the stall and slowly walked towards them with my hand outstretched. The mommy seemed to know she was now safe and took a step towards me with her nose reaching out to smell my hand. It was love at first sight, I believe, for the three of us. The bell rang to say the auction was starting, so I stroked her neck and said softly that I would see them a little later.

The bidding was very brisk for the donkey and her grey and white baby. It started at $300 and quickly ran up to $800. At this point, a lady sitting across the ring was the only bidder left besides myself. She looked at me to see if I was going to bid again. I couldn't believe the price had gone this high for a donkey, as usually you can buy them for a few hundred dollars. I hesitated for a second, and thought to myself, "You've gone this far, Pam, so keep going." Looking the auctioneer straight in the eye, I made my bid of $850. "Are there any more bids?" the auctioneer asked the crowd. No one responded. "Sold to Pam Dickson!" he said as he brought his hammer down on the desk.

I couldn't wait to get my dear little donkeys back home. As I was leaning over to pat them, a man who had a horse trailer said he would be happy to deliver them for me. Within fifteen minutes they were walking down the ramp of the trailer and happily grazing in their new paddock. Rosie and Teddy were to be their names.

In 1988, I built an addition onto the kennels to hold another fourteen kennels for larger dogs and decided to reconcrete the area I had put down years earlier by myself. It had served well, but now was the time to remodel the whole complex, including putting up new chainlink kennels throughout.

Teddy and Rosie
share a nibble off their favorite maple tree overlooking a fifty-acre pasture.

Charles Smith concreted the back of the kennels and built a covered roof, which went all the way around the outer length of the kennels. Each inside kennel has its own outdoor run looking over a fifty-acre pasture. New doors with windows replaced the old stable doors, and a veranda covers part of the shed row, which makes all the kennels very light, airy, and cozy.

I also remodeled the grooming salon with a new hot-water heater, a bathtub at waist level (so whoever is bathing a dog does not have to lean over), a washing machine, and kennels to put dogs in while they are awaiting their owners.

Over the years, I had taken photos of Rocky and Spotty and lots of wild animals, all of which I thought turned out quite well. I had the idea that perhaps clients would like to have their pets' photos taken while they were boarding. I mentioned it to several of my clients to get their reaction, and everyone was very enthusiastic.

Over in Manassas, a firm sold sheds in the skeleton stage, which would be finished off very nicely. Cliff, a man of many talents who helps me mow the grass, insulated and painted one of these sheds to make it into a studio. On one wall inside, a local artist painted a scene overlooking the fields as a backdrop for the photos.

When the dogs arrive at the kennels, most of the owners have brought treats for them to enjoy during their stay. This gave me the incentive to buy yet another shed, this one larger than the studio, measuring fifteen by twenty-five feet. Cliff insulated and paneled the inside with a light color, which made it appear more spacious. The building has six large windows, with fitted shutters on either side.

The shop isn't large, but it is big enough for me to handle anything that people would want to buy for their pets. Handmade collars and leads hang on the wall, and the shelves are filled with all kinds of biscuits, treats, shampoos, brushes, combs, wonderful handmade washable beds, and perfectly fitted coats.

I moved the office desk into the right-hand corner, which overlooks the flower garden and lawns. Everything at the kennels is very organized. I created a place for everything, and if there was weakness in design, I tried to turn it into a strength.

My last project was to pull down all the outside exercise runs. They still looked good, but I thought they had more than done their job, and it would be nice to have all new gates and fences. My heart sank a little as I watched two men demolishing my wire and posts, but then I began to smile when they had great difficulty in removing my extra-strong posts that I had put in twenty-three years ago.

Looking from the entrance over into the runs gives me a feeling of satisfaction, especially when there are many breeds of dogs wagging their tails or, so very often, barking with excitement when a client comes to visit.

As the finishing touch to the kennels' entrance, there stands a bell which was on the first American oil tanker, the S.S. *Lyman Stewart*, and is dated 1915. It was given to me by a friend and neighbor, Bud Little, whose wife Margaret's grandfather had owned the line.

Bud and Maggie had been top show riders in their younger days in Chicago and had moved to Middleburg to raise horses at their Heritage Farm-Thoroughbred yearlings to sell at the Saratoga auction sales, and driving horses. They began to raise Jack Russells many years ago and became one of the United States' leading breeders of these endearing dogs. Although Maggie has passed away, Bud keeps a real old-time farm, housing a variety of animals from potbellied pigs to chickens, ducks, sheep, and donkeys.

One day Bud had come to visit the kennels and sat on the steps after ringing the small English bell I had carried back from a visit home. He sat, and sat, since we did not hear the bell. When I finally did discover him sitting there, Bud said he would like to give me a bell that I would be able to hear. He promptly brought it over the very next day and had two of his farm workers dig a hole, put in a post, and erect the bell. He told me that when it was rung at Heritage Farm, it could be heard from one end to the other. At the kennels, it is a real showpiece, and we no longer neglect our visitors!

Entrance to Fursman Kennels.

Chapter 21

The Visit

The kennels have grown considerably over the years. Clients, both local and from many miles away, bring their pets to the "country club," as it is often called.

As you turn into my entrance, you can see the soft, rolling countryside and in the distance the Bull Run Mountains of Fauquier County. Just over my fence line to the right is Hickory Tree Farm, the home of beautiful Thoroughbred mares and foals, and in the spring I love to sit on the fence and watch the babies run and play with each other, showing off their boundless energy as they race around their large, neatly kept paddocks.

Driving down my lane gives you a look of true, natural beauty. Century-old oak and maple trees stand on either side, and a winding creek trickles under a narrow wooden bridge. Daffodils and daylilies flutter in the breeze in their own season, and beyond them is a covert for wild flowers and animals. Frequently foxes and deer can be seen crossing the drive, and rabbits and chipmunks show little fear of cars passing by.

Sometimes when I walk in this sunlit glade, the outside world seems far away, and any changes that the world has cared to make seem quite insignificant.

A little distance away from this quiet, unhurried haven is a stone entrance where, in the spring, I plant the varied colors of impatiens, while on the opposite side, water lilies bloom in a small goldfish pond. Frogs, too, enjoy this sanctuary and are completely unafraid as they sit on the lily pads sunning themselves.

On the right of the entrance near the kennels are two fields through which the creek continues its leisurely way. Here my two pet donkeys enjoy a restful life, grazing on the green lush grass and lazily watching the activities that go on around them. Their special treat in the afternoon is a large juicy carrot that Jody gives them, and if for some reason he is a few minutes late, they stand by the fence and complain, very loudly, until they attract his attention.

A little farther down the drive, in a superb setting of lawns and flower beds, which show the obvious English flavor, the atmosphere of the kennels is heightened by the presence of more ancient oak trees and shrubs.

As you come around the large circle in front of the office and kennels, dogwoods and flowering plum trees grow. Looking over the beauty of the scenery and its picturesque cottage is the horse stable, standing in a cluster of imposing poplar trees.

The grave of Rocky is nearby, in a large flower bed. I like to think he has seen and approved of all the changes that have occurred over the past years.

*There are many handsome frogs in the water lily pond,
and several varieties of beautiful hardy lilies.*

One thing that worried me in my earlier years in America was that I felt that my Dad did not know where I was living. I always imagined that when a person died, his soul went straight to heaven. One day, when I was on my tractor cutting grass near the kennels, in the shade of the oak trees, I happened to turn my head towards one of the trees by the kennels' entrance. And there, standing beneath the oak tree just twenty yards away, was my father. He was wearing his favorite sports coat and peaked cap and had his hands in the pockets of his grey flannel trousers. For a split second I forgot he had died. It happened just as if it were a normal thing for him to be standing watching me mowing the grass. Looking straight at me with a peaceful look on his face, he then simply vanished all too soon for me to speak to him.

Previously, if anyone told me they had experienced a vision such as mine, frankly, I never really believed them and thought it was a figment of their imagination.

Tears began to well in my eyes as I continued to drive my small tractor, making another sweep around the majestic oaks. My body began to tremble, but at the same time I felt at ease. My Dad had let me know he was all right, and that he knew I was, too.

Tomorrow, the weather has been forecast to be in the mid-70s with a clear blue sky. It would be a perfectly glorious day for me to drive the sixty miles south to Fredericksburg, where I heard a lady has some six-week-old German shepherd puppies for sale. Perhaps at these kennels, my endless search for a new puppy will come to an end.

Stone entrance in the spring.

Excerpted from *Who's Who of Dogs—Extraordinary Lives of Ordinary Dogs;* reprinted with the kind permission of the publisher.

Meet Robin Gookin, Middleburg, Virginia. Robin, a local boy, was born in a barn near Middleburg nearly fourteen years ago. His mother was a Jack Russell terrier and, although we haven't met his father, he must have been a big handsome boy because Robin developed into one of the strongest, best-looking, seventy-pound farm dogs around. His favorite activities are being taken out for a good run, rubbing in anything foul, and vacationing on Cape Cod. When he can't be with his master and mistress he goes happily to *Fursman Kennels (the canine Hot Springs),* where he is treated like a big shot and has lots of friends.